# THE BOND MARKET IN INDONESIA

## AN ASEAN+3 BOND MARKET GUIDE UPDATE

DECEMBER 2021

ADB

ASIAN DEVELOPMENT BANK

© 2021 Asian Development Bank
6 ADB Avenue, Mandaluyong City, 1550 Metro Manila, Philippines

www.adb.org

Some rights reserved. Published in 2021.

ISBN 978-92-9269-199-8 (print), 978-92-9269-200-1 (electronic), 978-92-9269-201-8 (ebook)
ISSN 2616-4663 (print), 2616-4671 (electronic)
Publication Stock No. TCS 210472-2
DOI: http://dx.doi.org/10.22617/TCS210472-2

The views expressed in this publication are those of the authors and do not necessarily reflect the views and policies of the Asian Development Bank (ADB) or its Board of Governors or the governments they represent.

ADB does not guarantee the accuracy of the data included in this publication and accepts no responsibility for any consequence of their use. The mention of specific companies or products of manufacturers does not imply that they are endorsed or recommended by ADB in preference to others of a similar nature that are not mentioned.

By making any designation of or reference to a particular territory or geographic area, or by using the term "economy" in this document, ADB does not intend to make any judgments as to the legal or other status of any territory or area.

Corrigenda to ADB publications may be found at http://www.adb.org/publications/corrigenda.

Notes:
In this report, international standards for naming conventions—International Organization for Standardization (ISO) 3166 for economy codes and ISO 4217 for currency codes—are used to reflect the discussions of the ASEAN+3 Bond Market Forum to promote and support implementation of international standards in financial transactions in the region. ASEAN+3 comprises the Association of Southeast Asian Nations (ASEAN) plus the People's Republic of China, Japan, and the Republic of Korea.

The economies of ASEAN+3 as defined in ISO 3166 include Brunei Darussalam (BN; BRN); Cambodia (KH; KHM); the People's Republic of China (CN; CHN); Hong Kong, China (HK; HKG); Indonesia (ID; IDN); Japan (JP; JPN); the Republic of Korea (KR; KOR); the Lao People's Democratic Republic (LA; LAO); Malaysia (MY; MYS); Myanmar (MM; MMR); the Philippines (PH; PHL); Singapore (SG; SGP); Thailand (TH; THA); and Viet Nam (VN; VNM).

The currencies of ASEAN+3 as defined in ISO 4217 include the Brunei dollar (BND), Cambodian riel (KHR), Chinese renminbi (CNY), Hong Kong dollar (HKD), Indonesian rupiah (IDR), Japanese yen (JPY), Korean won (KRW), Lao kip (LAK), Malaysian ringgit (MYR), Myanmar kyat (MMK), Philippine peso (PHP), Singapore dollar (SGD), Thai baht (THB), and Vietnamese dong (VND).

ADB recognizes "Hong Kong" as Hong Kong, China and "Korea" as the Republic of Korea.

# Contents

Note: The chapter and section numbering reflect that of the *ASEAN+3 Bond Market Guide 2017 for Indonesia*, and includes only the chapters and sections being updated.

# Tables and Figures

# Acknowledgments

The *ASEAN+3 Bond Market Guide for Indonesia* was published in August 2017.[1] While Indonesia's Capital Market Law has remained unchanged, the regulatory authorities and market institutions have carried out a significant review of and revisions to the regulatory framework in the years since, adding investor types, issuance methods, and new instruments, and adjusting market features ranging from credit rating to reporting. As such, an update of the original *ASEAN+3 Bond Market Guide for Indonesia* has become necessary.

Interested parties will appreciate the information on the introduction of a professional investors concept and offerings that target those investors. Indonesia has also been spearheading the issuance of sovereign green *sukuk* (Islamic bonds), while regulatory authorities and market institutions are increasingly anchoring the application of technology in regulations and rules; examples include crowdfunding of debt and other securities, the introduction of issuance and alternative electronic trading platforms, and the conduct of voting and meetings via approved platforms.

The ASEAN+3 Bond Market Forum (ABMF) Sub-Forum 1 team wishes to thank Bank Indonesia, the Indonesia Financial Services Authority, the Ministry of Finance of Indonesia, Indonesia Stock Exchange, Indonesia Clearing and Guarantee Corporation, Indonesia Central Securities Depository, the Indonesia Securities Pricing Corporation, as well as ABMF International Experts including Deutsche Bank AG and PT. Bank HSBC Indonesia for their inputs and review of this update note.

In addition, the ABMF team acknowledges the inputs from Indonesian bond market participants who are not ABMF members, including law firm Mochtar Karuwin Komar, which contributed its time and expertise in support of this update note.

No part of this update note represents the official views or opinions of any institution that participated in this activity as an ABMF member, observer, or expert. The ABMF Sub-Forum 1 team bears sole responsibility for the contents of this update note.

This update note and those relating to other ASEAN+3 bond markets are available for download from *AsianBondsOnline*.[2]

December 2021

ASEAN+3 Bond Market Forum

---

[1] Asian Development Bank (ADB). 2017. *ASEAN+3 Bond Market Guide 2017 for Indonesia*. Manila. https://asianbondsonline.adb.org/abmg.php#ino-2017.
[2] Asian Bonds Online. https://asianbondsonline.adb.org.

# Abbreviations

| | |
|---|---|
| ABMF | ASEAN+3 Bond Market Forum |
| ADB | Asian Development Bank |
| ASEAN | Association of Southeast Asian Nations |
| ASEAN+3 | ASEAN plus the People's Republic of China, Japan, and the Republic of Korea |
| BBF | Basket Bond Futures |
| BI | Bank Indonesia |
| CICERO | Center for International Climate and Environmental Research–Oslo |
| CIS | collective investment schemes |
| CRA | credit rating agency |
| CWLS | cash *waqf*-linked *sukuk* |
| DGT | Directorate General of Taxation |
| IBPA | Indonesia Bond Pricing Agency (now PHEI) |
| ICMA | International Capital Market Association |
| IDR | Indonesian rupiah |
| IDX | Indonesia Stock Exchange |
| IGBF | Indonesia Government Bond Futures |
| KPEI | Kliring Penjaminan Efek Indonesia (Indonesia Clearing and Guarantee Corp.) |
| KSEI | Kustodian Sentral Efek Indonesia (Indonesia Central Securities Depository) |
| MOF | Ministry of Finance |
| MPSJKI | Indonesian Financial Services Sector Master Plan (2021–2025) |
| OJK | Otoritas Jasa Keuangan (Indonesia Financial Services Authority) |
| PHEI | Penilai Harga Efek Indonesia (Indonesia Securities Pricing Corporation) |
| PLTE | Penerima Laporan Transaksi (Efek Securities Transaction Reporting Platform |
| PPA | Penyelenggara Pasar Alternatif (Alternative Market Organizer) |
| SDG | Sustainable Development Goals |
| SID | Single Investor Identification |
| SN-PPPK | Strategi Nasional Pengembangan dan Pendalaman Pasar Keuangan (National Strategy for Financial Market Development, 2018–2024) |
| SPE | Sistem Pelaporan Emiten atau Perusahaan Publik (Reporting System for Issuers and Public Companies) |
| SPPA | Sistem Penyelenggara Pasar Alternatif (Alternative Market Platform) |
| SPRINT | Sistem Perizinan dan Registrasi Terintegrasi (Integrated Licensing and Registration System) |
| SRO | self-regulatory organization |
| USD | United States dollar (ISO code) |

USD1 = IDR14,462 as of 30 September 2021 (Jakarta Interbank Spot Dollar Rate)

# Overview

## A. Introduction

Indonesia's Financial Services Authority (OJK) has prioritized the development of the corporate bond market ecosystem by building strong domestic investor and issuer bases. OJK views that strengthening such domestic bases is important for the stability of the capital market and Indonesia's overall monetary, fiscal, and financial systems.

In pursuit of these objectives, OJK and the market institutions—such as the Indonesia Stock Exchange (IDX), Indonesia Clearing and Guarantee Corp (IDClear), and Indonesia Central Securities Depository (KSEI)—issued many new or amended regulations and rules since the publication of the *ASEAN+3 Bond Market Guide for Indonesia* in 2017 that have augmented the regulatory framework for the bond and capital markets at large.[3] The revised or new regulations range from consolidating credit rating requirements and improving disclosure to new instruments and issuance types. They have also subsumed or superseded regulations originating during the capital market's supervision by either Bapepam or Bapepam-LK. Major new or revised regulations and rules, and the market developments they support, are explained in this update note in the context of the chapters and sections in the *ASEAN+3 Bond Market Guide for Indonesia* that they relate to.

New market features and functions include the introduction of a professional investors concept (Chapter III.N) and triparty repurchase agreement (repo) services by a market institution (Chapter IV.G). IDX launched bond-related futures contracts on its market in May 2017 (Chapter IV.I) and listed the first green bond in 2018 (Chapter III.I).

The use and application of technology has played an ever-increasing role in the Indonesian bond market—as evidenced by a dedicated government portal for electronic subscription for retail government securities, both sovereign bonds and *sukuk*; the inception of crowdfunding organizers and their platforms for the issuance of securities (including debt securities); and also the number of regulations enabling electronic submission of issuance documentation and disclosure information to authorities and self-regulatory organizations (SROs). New issuance types and channels are explained in Chapter III.E.

The number and variations of debt instruments and *sukuk* issued by both the Government of Indonesia and corporate issuers has also increased further (Chapter III.B) and resulted in a number of international firsts, such as the first sovereign green *sukuk* issued in 2018 and the first EUR-denominated, sovereign Sustainable Development Goals (SDG) bond in September 2021 (Chapter X.A). ]/issuance segment in line with increasing demand from investors and the coordinated approach toward more sustainable finance options among Indonesian policy makers.

---

[3] ASEAN+3 refers to the 10 members of the Association of Southeast Asian Nations (ASEAN) plus the People's Republic of China, Japan, and the Republic of Korea. Asian Development Bank. *ASEAN+3 Bond Market Guide for Indonesia.* 2017. https://asianbondsonline.adb.org/abmg.php#ino-2017.

The particular focus on Sharia instruments and the increasing number of *sukuk* varieties prompted IDX to distinguish listing rules for *sukuk* from those for conventional debt securities, owing also to the special characteristics of the Islamic principles underlying *sukuk* and their disclosure practices.

To frame and support capital market development, the Government of Indonesia published its *National Strategy for Financial Market Development, 2018–2024* (see section E of this chapter), while Bank Indonesia (BI) published its own *Blueprint for Money Market Development, 2025* (see section F of this chapter). In addition to strengthening the regulatory framework for the bond and capital markets, OJK also issued the *Sustainable Finance Roadmap Phase II (2021–2025)* that integrates sustainable financing approaches across instruments and industries (see section H of this chapter).

These market initiatives and changes to the regulatory framework contributed to a significant increase since 2016 in the amount of IDR-denominated debt securities and *sukuk* outstanding in Indonesia, the last year for which data was included in the *ASEAN+3 Bond Market Guide for Indonesia* (Figure 1.1). In addition, the Government of Indonesia's response to the coronavirus disease (COVID-19) pandemic resulted in a 119.6% year-on-year increase in sovereign bond and *sukuk* issuance in 2020 to IDR956.3 trillion.[4]

**Figure 1.1: Local Currency Bonds Outstanding in Indonesia**
(USD billion)

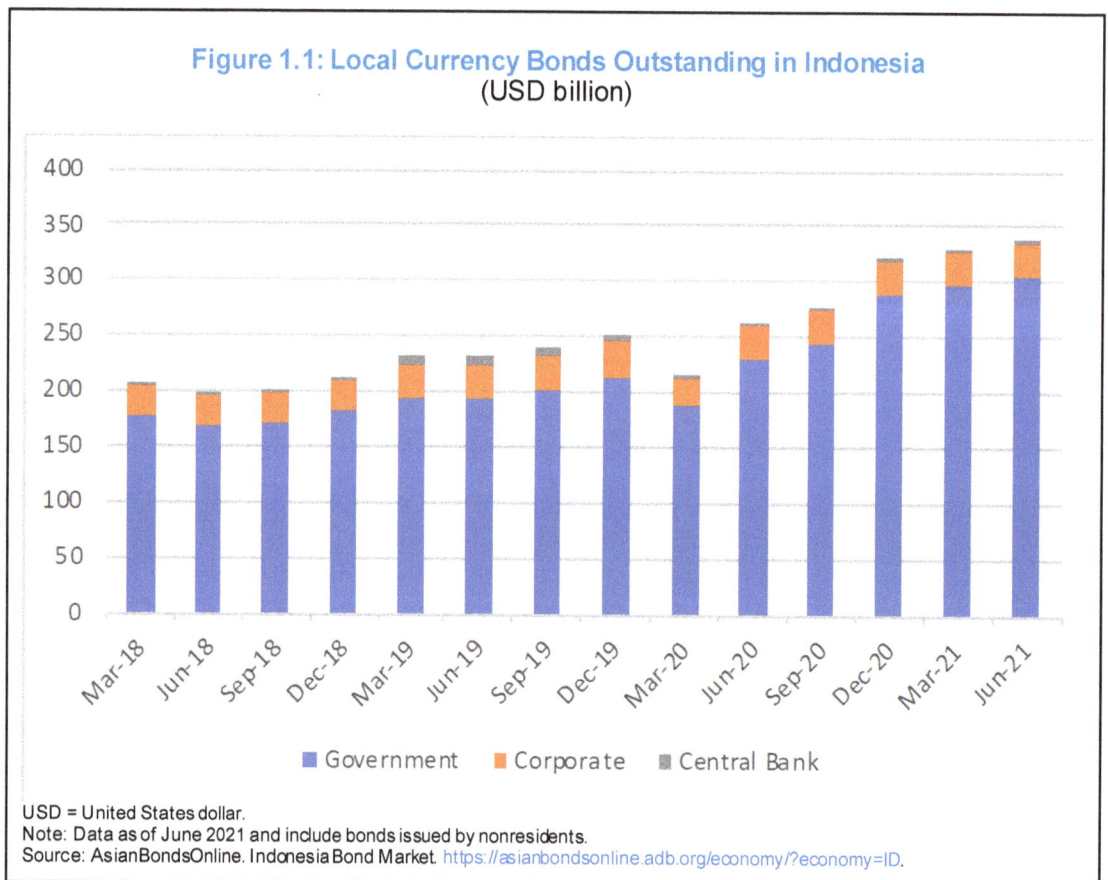

USD = United States dollar.
Note: Data as of June 2021 and include bonds issued by nonresidents.
Source: AsianBondsOnline. Indonesia Bond Market. https://asianbondsonline.adb.org/economy/?economy=ID.

At the end of June 2021, the total outstanding amount of local currency bonds and *sukuk* was nearly exactly double the amount at the end of June 2016. While the bond market continues to be dominated by sovereign issuances, outstanding corporate

---

[4] Total issuance amounts for 2019 and 2020 are based on the January 2020 and January 2021 editions of the Ministry of Finance's *Determination of the State Budget*, respectively. The reports are available in Bahasa Indonesia from the Ministry of Finance website at https://www.kemenkeu.go.id/publikasi/apbn-kita/.

bonds and *sukuk* have increased by more than 50% in the past 4.5 years. Foreign investors held IDR997.41 trillion in IDR-denominated bonds and *sukuk* as of 21 December 2020, reflecting a decline of about 6% from a year earlier.[5]

In addition to bond market information available on *AsianBondsOnline*, comprehensive data on outstanding bonds and *sukuk*—including their issuances, composition, and trading volumes, as well as a breakdown by investor type—are available on the websites of BI, IDX, and other market institutions (see Chapter VII for appropriate links).

## D.    Regional Cooperation

### 2.    Bilateral Cooperation of the Indonesia Central Securities Depository

To improve its regional and international cooperation framework, KSEI entered into bilateral cooperation agreements with, among others, the Central Depository (Pte.) Limited of Singapore; Japan Securities Depository Center, Inc.; Korea Securities Depository; Central Securities Depository of Iran; Merkezi Kayit Kurulusu A.S., Turkish Central Securities Depository; and Thailand Securities Depository Co., Ltd. The expanded cooperation is expected to support KSEI's activities in the Indonesian capital market as well as international markets.

## E.    National Strategy for Financial Market Development, 2018–2024

The Ministry of Finance (MOF), BI, and OJK co-authored the *National Strategy for Financial Market Development, 2018–2024*, published on 15 January 2019. The strategy is officially known as the National Financial Market Development and Deepening Strategy (SN-PPPK). The bond market is one of six focus market segments named in SN-PPPK. `

According to the authoring institutions, the depth of the financial markets in Indonesia is not yet on par with peer jurisdictions, as evidenced by the infrastructure funding gap, which is massive and necessitates bond and other instrument issuance on a regular basis.

SN-PPPK identifies three pillars of financial market development and defines seven elements of the targeted financial market ecosystem for Indonesia. SN-PPPK further lists and discusses in great detail eight objectives for the development of the government bond market and seven objectives for the corporate bond market, plus additional goals for the money market; each objective or goal was assigned to one or more pillars.

SN-PPPK is to be implemented in three phases: (i) strengthening the foundations in 2018–2019, (ii) an acceleration of market development in 2020–2022, and (iii) a deepening phase in 2023–2024. Each phase contains key performance indicators to be achieved, ranging from indicators for growth and absolute size for turnover and volume to the composition of financial instruments. An increase in the number of issuers and the broadening of the investor base is a common goal in all three phases. Please also see subsequent sections of this chapter for information on the master plans and road maps of individual market authorities as a follow-up to SN-PPPK.

---

[5] Some information compiled from reports in the public domain.

An English language version of the *National Strategy for Financial Market Development, 2018–2024* is available from the website of BI and other market authorities.[6]

## F. Indonesian Financial Services Sector Master Plan, 2021–2025

OJK authored the Indonesian Financial Services Sector Master Plan, 2021–2025 (MPSJKI). The MPSJKI represents a continuation of the Indonesian Financial Services Sector Master Plan, 2015–2019 published in January 2016. The MPSJKI, 2021–2025 was intended to be effective in early 2020 but due to the disruptions caused by COVID-19, it was carried out in separate stages; the complete MPSJKI, 2021–2025 was eventually published in December 2020.

OJK considered it necessary to formulate the MPSJKI, 2021–2025 to address various conditions and challenges in the financial services sector and build on the achievements and market developments guided by the previous version. For the bond and capital markets, the previous MPSJKI had delivered, among other achievements, a more robust regulatory framework, the integration of fintech into that framework though initiatives such as equity crowdfunding, as well as new instruments and issuance types. OJK will use the MPSJKI, 2021–2025 as a basic framework for the strategic direction of its policies for the financial services sector.[7] The MPSJKI, 2021–2025 also integrates elements from presidential directives and objectives of national development agendas. Furthermore, OJK recognizes that economic and financial activities in Indonesia are increasingly integrated with the initiatives of the ASEAN Economic Community.

In relation to the bond and capital markets, the MPSJKI, 2021–2025 identifies challenges that include a limited range of sustainable financing instruments and related incentives; a lack of financing options for micro, small, and medium-sized enterprises; as well as the need to obtain and analyze more data to aid effective market supervision. The MPSJKI, 2021–2025 contains broad policy objectives to address these challenges. One of the pillars of OJK's framework is digital transformation acceleration, including the development of a regulatory framework that supports a digital financial sector ecosystem.

An English language version of the MPSJKI, 2021–2025 is available for download from the OJK website.[8]

## G. Blueprint for Money Market Development, 2025

BI published its *Blueprint for Money Market Development, 2025* in December 2020. It is referenced as the BPPU 2025 in the document and the public domain at large. The BPPU 2025 supports the guidance of the SN-PPPK policy framework and seeks to address the current and future challenges faced by BI as both the central bank and a key component of Indonesia's financial market infrastructure. The BPPU 2025 is organized into five visions, with specific deliverables under each one.

---

[6] Bank Indonesia. 2018. *National Strategy for Financial Market Development, 2018–2024.* https://www.bi.go.id/en/publikasi/kajian/Pages/Strategi-Nasional-Pengembangan-dan-Pendalaman-Pasar-Keuangan-2018-2024.aspx.

[7] Text adapted from the MPSJKI, 2021–2025 and reports in the public domain.

[8] OJK. 2020. *The Indonesian Financial Services Sector Master Plan to Recover the National Economy and Enhance the Financial Services Sector Resiliency and Competitiveness 2021–2025.* Indonesia Financial Services Authority. https://ojk.go.id/id/berita-dan-kegiatan/publikasi/Documents/Pages/Master-Plan-Sektor-Jasa-Keuangan-Indonesia-2021-2025/The%20Indonesian%20Financial%20Services%20Sector%20Master%20Plan%202021-2025.pdf.

Among the key deliverables identified in the BPPU 2025 are the further development of the repo remarket to strengthen the effectiveness of monetary policy transmission, development of sustainable and green financing as an alternative financing source, and development of long-term hedging instruments. Specific objectives include the use of a matching system for money market transactions and a shift from voice trading to electronic trading. BI will also modernize its depository and settlement system and its auction platform for government securities to accommodate all auction mechanisms and price allocation methods.

An English language version of the BPPU 2025 is available for download from the BI website. [9]

## H.    Sustainable Finance Roadmap Phase II (2021–2025)

OJK launched the *Sustainable Finance Roadmap Phase II (2021–2025)* in January 2021.

The *Sustainable Finance Roadmap Phase I (2015–2019)* aimed to increase the understanding and capacity of financial services sector actors to move toward a low-carbon economy. Phase I achieved several milestones, such as introducing sustainable finance principles, establishing relevant regulations, identifying numerous sustainable business criteria, developing an incentive scheme, and conducting a series of training programs for the financial industry.

Priorities expressed in Phase II of the roadmap include the development of a green taxonomy, which aims to classify sustainable financing and investment activities in Indonesia; the implementation of environmental, social, and governance aspects into risk management; and the development of a program for innovative green schemes to enhance the role of the financial industry in sustainable financing. The identified goals range from green certification of products and services to increased demand for sustainable financing products and expanded investments in information technology and capacity building to be achieved through regulatory and fiscal approaches (e.g., incentives). [10]

For further information, the *Sustainable Finance Roadmap Phase II (2021–2025)* is available as a bilingual document in Bahasa Indonesia and English from the OJK website. [11]

---

[9] BI. 2020. *Blueprint for Money Market Development 2025–Bank Indonesia: Building a Modern and Advanced Money Market in a Digital Era.* https://www.bi.go.id/en/publikasi/kajian/Documents/Blueprint-For-Money-Market-Development-2025.pdf.

[10] Text in part adapted from OJK. 2021. *Sustainable Finance Roadmap Phase II (2021–2025): The Future of Finance.* Indonesia Financial Services Authority. Jakarta.

[11] OJK. *Sustainable Finance Roadmap Phase II (2021–2025).* https://www.ojk.go.id/id/berita-dan-kegiatan/publikasi/Documents/Pages/Roadmap-Keuangan-Berkelanjutan-Tahap-II-%282021-2025%29/Roadmap%20Keuangan%20Berkelanjutan%20Tahap%20II%20%282021-2025%29.pdf.

# II

# Legal and Regulatory Framework

This chapter reviews the significant changes or updates to rules and regulations, regulatory processes, and other official prescriptions by regulatory authorities and market institutions in the Indonesian bond and capital markets since the publication of the *ASEAN+3 Bond Market Guide for Indonesia*.

## B. English Translation

OJK and market institutions—such as IDX, IDClear, and KSEI—have promulgated and published a large number of new regulations and rules, and revised and augmented existing regulations and rules, since 2017.

OJK and the market institutions continue their work of making available the English translations of all regulations and rules on their websites for the easy reference of market watchers and interested parties. At the same time, law and accounting firms increasingly feature practical English summaries of new regulations and rules on their websites or on portals covering legal subjects.

## C. Legislative Structure

Law No. 8 of 1995 on the Capital Market (Capital Market Law) has remained unchanged. To meet market expectations and facilitate market development objectives, OJK addressed subjects not covered in the Capital Market Law through the issuance of new regulations. In addition, OJK has been working toward updating or augmenting rules and regulations originating during the periods of Bapepam and (subsequently) Bapepam-LK supervision.

Table 2.1 has been updated to highlight regulations with a focus or impact on the bond and *sukuk* market that were introduced since the publication of the *ASEAN+3 Bond Market Guide for Indonesia* in 2017. Most of these new regulations will be referenced or reviewed in detail in the relevant chapters and sections of this update note, while preexisting regulations are shown in the table if they are also referenced in this document.

**Table 2.1: Examples of Securities Market Legislation or Regulations by Legislative Tier**

| Legislative Tier | Content or Significant Examples |
| --- | --- |
| Constitution of Indonesia | Principles, Rights, and Obligations |
| Laws (key legislation) | <ul><li>Law No. 11 of 2020 (Omnibus Law on Job Creation) [NEW]</li><li>Law No. 21 of 2011 on Otoritas Jasa Keuangan</li><li>Law No. 6 of 2009 on Bank Indonesia</li><li>Law No. 21 of 2008 on Sharia (Islamic) Banking</li><li>Law No. 8 of 1995 on the Capital Market</li></ul> |
| Regulations | <ul><li>OJK Regulation No. 16/POJK.04/2021 Concerning Amendment of OJK Regulation No. 57/POJK.04/2020 Concerning Offering of Securities through Crowdfunding Services Based on Information Technology (enacted 25 August 2021, promulgated 26 August 2021) [NEW]</li><li>OJK Regulation No. 3/POJK.04/2021 Concerning the Implementation of Activities in the Capital Market (enacted and promulgated 22 February 2021) [NEW]</li><li>OJK Regulation No. 57/POJK.04/2020 Concerning Offering of Securities through Crowdfunding Services Based on Information Technology (enacted 10 December 2020, promulgated 11 December 2020) [NEW]</li><li>OJK Regulation No. 53/POJK.04/2020 Concerning Securities Account at Custodian (enacted 3 December 2020, promulgated 11 December 2020) [NEW]</li><li>OJK Regulation No. 49/POJK.04/2020 Concering Rating of Debt Securities and/or Sukuk (enacted 3 December, promulgated 11 December 2020) [NEW]</li><li>OJK Regulation No. 41/POJK.04/2020 Concerning Implementation of Electronic Public Offering Activities of Equity Securities, Debt Securities and/or Sukuk (enacted 1 July 2020, promulgated 2 July 2020) [NEW]</li><li>OJK Regulation No. 32/POJK.04/2020 Concerning Securities Derivatives Contracts (enacted 27 April 2020, promulgated 6 May 2020) [NEW]</li><li>Minister of Finance Regulation No. 27 of 2020 Concerning the Sale of Retail Government Securities [NEW]</li><li>OJK Regulation No. 20/POJK.04/2020 Concerning Trustee Contracts for Debt Securities and/or Sukuk (enacted 22 April 2020, promulgated 23 April 2020) [NEW]</li><li>OJK Regulation No. 19/POJK.04/2020 Concerning Commercial Banks Conducting Activities as Trustees (enacted 22 April 2020, promulgated 23 April 2020) [NEW]</li><li>OJK Regulation No. 30/POJK.04/2019 Concerning Issuance of Debt Securities and/or Sukuk Not Through a Public Offering (enacted and promulgated on 29 November 2019) [NEW]</li><li>OJK Regulation No. 8/POJK.04/2019 Concerning Alternative Market Organizers (enacted 19 February 2019, promulgated 21 February 2021) [NEW]</li><li>OJK Regulation No. 11/POJK.04/2018 Concerning Public Offering of Debt Securities and/or Sukuk to Professional Investors (enacted and promulgated 1 August 2018) [NEW]</li><li>OJK Regulation No. 7/POJK.04/2018 Concerning Submission of Reports via the Electronic Reporting System for Issuers or Public Companies (enacted and promulgated 25 April 2018) [NEW]</li><li>OJK Regulation No. 61/POJK.04/2017 Concerning Registration Statement Documents for Public Offering of Municipal Bonds and/or Municipal Sukuk (enacted 21 December 2017, promulgated 22 December 2017) [NEW]</li></ul> |

| Legislative Tier | Content or Significant Examples |
|---|---|
|  | • OJK Regulation No. 60/POJK.04/2017 Concerning the Issuance and the Terms of Green Bond (enacted 21 December 2017, promulgated 22 December 2017) [NEW]<br>• OJK Regulation No. 58/POJK.04/2017 Concerning Electronic Submission of Registration Statement or Electronic Submission of Corporate Action (enacted 6 December 2017, promulgated 8 December 2017) [NEW]<br>• OJK Regulation No. 9/POJK.04/2017 Concerning Prospectus Form and Content and Brief Prospectus for Debt Securities Public Offering (enacted and promulgated 14 March 2017)<br>• OJK Regulation No. 7/POJK.04/2017 Concerning Document of Registration Statement for Equity and Debt/Sukuk Securities Public Offering (enacted and promulgated 14 March 2017)<br>• OJK Regulation No. 36/POJK.04/2014) Concerning Shelf Registration (enacted and promulgated 8 December 2014) |
| Circular Letters, Decisions, Instructions | • IDX Circular Letter SE-00006/BEI/10-2019 Regarding Procedure for the Submission of Electronic Report by Listed Companies (28 October 2019) [NEW]<br>• Chief Executive of Capital Market Supervisor Decision Number Kep-52/D.04/2019 Regarding Appointment of IDX as a System Provider of Electronic Reporting for Issuer and Public Companies [NEW]<br>• OJK Circular Letter No. 33/SEOJK/04/2015 Concerning Global Master Repurchase Agreement Indonesia (enacted 23 November 2015, effective 1 January 2016) |
| SRO Regulations | • IDX Rule Number I-G Concerning Sukuk Listing (effective 26 March 2021) [NEW]<br>• IDX Rule Number I-E Concerning Obligation to Submit Information (effective 1 February 2021) [NEW]<br>• IDX Decree SE-00004/BEI/01-2021 on Trading Parameters of Debt Securities and Sukuk in the Alternative Trading Platform (19 January 2021, effective 8 February 2021) [NEW]<br>• IDX Rule Number II-E Concerning Futures Contract Trading (effective 7 December 2020) [NEW]<br>• KPEI Regulation Number III-2 on Clearing and Guarantee of Settlement of Securities Futures Contract Transactions (effective 27 November 2020) [NEW]<br>• IDX Decree KEP-000093/BEI/11-2020 Regarding Securities Trading Regulations through the Alternative Trading Platform (9 November 2020) [NEW]<br>• KSEI Regulation Number II-B Regarding Registration of Debt Securities and/or Sukuk at KSEI (15 October 2020) [NEW]<br>• KSEI Regulation Number V-D Regarding Free of Payment Instruction for the Book-Entry of Securities at KSEI (29 July 2020) [NEW]<br>• IDX Decree KEP-00038/BEI/05-2020 on Amendment to Rule Number I-B Concerning Listing of Debt Securities (20 May 2020) [NEW]<br>• IDX Decree SE-00005/BEI/09-2019 on Procedure for the Submission of Report in the Form of Electronic Document and/or Electronic Data by the Securities Exchange Member (effective 2 September 2019) [NEW]<br>• KPEI Regulation Number X-2 Regarding Triparty Repo Facility (effective 28 February 2019) [NEW]<br>• KSEI Regulation Number I-C Regarding Securities Sub-Account (22 December 2017) [NEW]<br>• KPEI Regulation KEP-013/DIR/KPEI/0517 Regarding Retail State Bond Trading Clearing in Electronic Trading Platform (26 May 2017) [NEW] |

IDX = Indonesia Stock Exchange, KPEI = Kliring Penjaminan Efek Indonesia (Indonesia Clearing and Guarantee Corporation), KSEI = Kustodian Sentral Efek Indonesia (Indonesia Central Securities Depository), OJK = Otoritas Jasa Keungan (Financial Services Authority), SRO = self-regulatory organization.
Note: Regulations have been sorted chronologically beginning with the most recent promulgations.
Source: ASEAN+3 Bond Market Forum Sub-Forum 1 team based on publicly available information.

## E.    Regulatory Framework for Debt Securities

Following the introduction of regulations for the issuance of debt securities and/or *sukuk* via private placement, effective 1 June 2020, all issuance types of corporate bonds and *sukuk*, in the bond market in Indonesia, including green and sustainability instruments, are under the purview of OJK.

While issuance via public offerings and public offerings to professional investors are subject to OJK review and approval, issuance via private placement only requires the filing of the prescribed issuance documentation with OJK prior to issuance.

Pursuant to the new regulations, private placements need to be registered and deposited with KSEI, while debt securities or *sukuk* issued via crowdfunding platforms may be deposited with KSEI (in case of scripless crowdfunded securities) or a custodian. Listings on IDX now include debt instruments issued via either a public offering or a public offering to professional investors, as well as green and sustainability bonds, municipal bonds, and those issued by small and medium-sized enterprises. IDX also now separates the listing rules between *sukuk* and conventional bonds to better cater to the specifics of each instrument type.

In addition, OJK regulated the concept of Alternative Market Organizers, i.e., the ability to establish and operate formalized alternative trading venues for government and corporate bonds and *sukuk* in the over-the-counter (OTC) market. Promulgated on 19 February 2019, OJK Regulation No. 8/POJK.04/2019 Concerning Alternative Market Organizers contains provisions on the activities, capital, and shareholders of potential Alternative Market Organizers (PPA), and prescribes the licensing and operational practices for PPA.

The role of BI as the setter of regulations for open market operations and Indonesia's foreign exchange regime remains unchanged.

## F.    Debt Securities Issuance Regulatory Processes

With the introduction of the professional investors concept in 2018, OJK also made available the issuance of a public offering to professional investors, while giving concessions to issuers—please see section F.5.a for an explanation of the terminology used in this document—or those that had previously issued debt securities or *sukuk* via a public offering. At the same time, a public offering to professional investors principally follows the regulatory process previously established for public offerings, including the submission of a Registration Statement and the need for OJK to declare it effective.

In 2020, OJK added a regulatory process for the issuance of debt securities or *sukuk* via private placement, formalizing initial disclosure through the filing of issuance documentation with OJK prior to issuance. A Registration Statement is not required, and OJK will not review the quality of the contents or approve the documentation submitted, but will only check the documents for completeness and compliance with regulations. Depending on the nature of the entity issuing via a private placement, the use of an arranger and monitoring agent may be mandated, with OJK receiving reports on such a private placement during its tenor.

Listing eligibility and approval are determined by IDX on the basis of updated or new listing rules that now distinguish between *sukuk* and conventional debt instruments, and also extend to prescriptions for electronic submission and specific standard formats for disclosure information.

Only the new or adjusted regulatory processes are reviewed in detail in the subsequent sections of this update note.

### 1.    Regulatory Processes by Type of Issuing Entity

The introduction of issuance via a public offering to professional investors did not come with a new regulatory process, as the new issuance type follows the overall prescriptions for public offerings, requiring the submission of a Registration Statement and approval from OJK; however, the process itself contains concessions for eligible issuers (see also new section 9).

While the actual regulatory process for the issuance of debt securities or *sukuk* via a private placement does not differ by offeror type as such—all offerors need only submit their issuance documentation prior to issuance—the nature of an offeror does have implications for the mandatory appointment of service providers and the need to obtain a credit rating. Details of these distinctions are further explained in section 5 of this chapter.

The issuance of a private placement by a nonresident entity (other than a supranational institution) without prior issuance experience (and corresponding disclosure) in Indonesia is not possible.

### 3.    Regulatory Process in Case of a Nonresident Issuer

A nonresident entity may issue debt securities or *sukuk* via a public offering and, in doing so, would be considered an "issuer" and subject to the same obligations and regulatory process as a domestic entity.[12]

Once considered an issuer, a nonresident entity would also be able to offer debt securities or *sukuk* via a private placement, provided that the debt securities previously issued via a public offering remain outstanding (If the Issuer had only issued debt securities or *sukuk*) and, hence, represent ongoing disclosure obligations in the Indonesian market. There is no distinction in the regulatory process for private placements between issuers that are resident or nonresident entities.

A nonresident entity without previous debt securities issuances via a public offering in Indonesia will not be able to issue debt securities or *sukuk* via a private placement, with the exception of supranational institutions.

Please also see section K in this chapter for any applicable new limitations on nonresidents, or see section K in Chapter II of the *ASEAN+3 Bond Market Guide for Indonesia* for a complete review of limitations applicable to nonresidents.

### 4.    Regulatory Process for Public Offerings

The promulgation of OJK Regulation No. 11/POJK.04/2018 concerning Public Offering of Debt Securities and/or Sukuk to Professional Investors in August 2018 added an issuance type specific to professional investors to bond issuances via a public offering. However, while the new issuance variant comes with some concessions, the regulatory process for public offerings to general or all investors remains unchanged.

---

[12] In the taxonomy for capital-market-related terms used by OJK, the term "issuer" denotes an entity having issued debt securities or *sukuk* (in fact any securities including equity securities) via a public offering, thereby having been subject to formal disclosure obligations in the capital market.

To highlight and better distinguish the regulatory process for public offerings of debt securities and/or *sukuk* to professional investors, a summary of the differences and concessions is provided in section 9 of this chapter.

The title of and regulatory process flow in Figure 2.1 was adjusted and the figure moved here since it now only represents part of the regulatory processes in the Indonesian bond market. The listing of debt securities or *sukuk* issued via a public offering, including a public offering to professional investors, remains optional; however, if a listing is sought and listing approval cannot be obtained, the entire public offering will be considered null and void.

**Figure 2.1: Regulatory Process Map—Issuance via Public Offering in Indonesia**

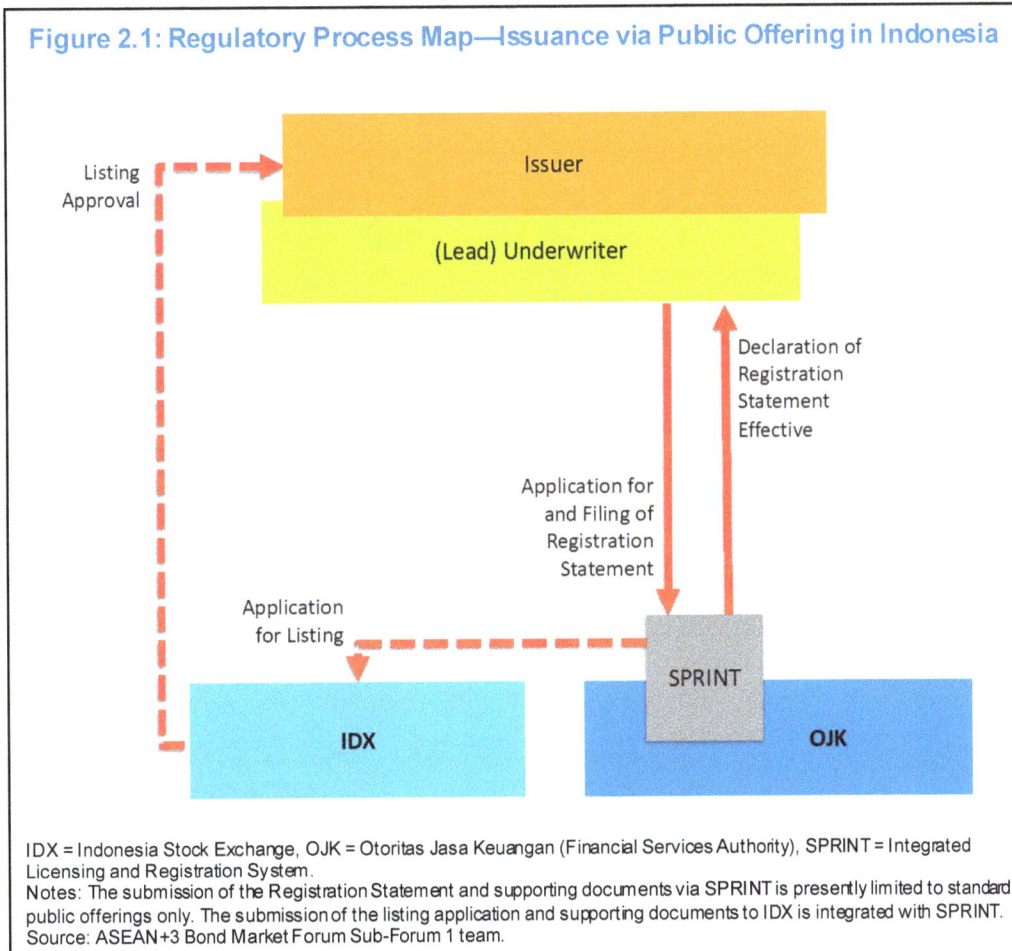

IDX = Indonesia Stock Exchange, OJK = Otoritas Jasa Keuangan (Financial Services Authority), SPRINT = Integrated Licensing and Registration System.
Notes: The submission of the Registration Statement and supporting documents via SPRINT is presently limited to standard public offerings only. The submission of the listing application and supporting documents to IDX is integrated with SPRINT.
Source: ASEAN+3 Bond Market Forum Sub-Forum 1 team.

Following the promulgation on 8 December 2017 of OJK Regulation No. 58/POJK.04/2017 Concerning Electronic Submission of Registration Statement or Electronic Submission of Corporate Action, and its effective date of 8 June 2018, the Registration Statement for a public offering of debt securities or *sukuk* and all documents that are an integral part of the Registration Statement need to be submitted to OJK electronically, via upload to OJK's Integrated Licensing and Registration System (SPRINT). In the event an upload cannot be performed, the Registration Statement needs to be submitted manually, i.e., sent via email or delivered directly to OJK on a data storage device.

Notwithstanding the electronic submission of the Registration Statement to OJK, the issuer will still need to submit up to five printed copies of the prospectus to OJK within 15 working days from the distribution of the issued debt securities or *sukuk* under prevailing regulations for the registration of a public offering of securities.

The electronic submission was further formalized by OJK with a dedicated system in 2018. For details about the reporting system implemented by OJK, the electronic submission process, as well as data practices, please refer to section 6 in this chapter.

## 5. Regulatory Process for Private Placements [NEW]

The introduction of OJK Regulation No. 30/POJK.04/2019 Concerning Issuance of Debt Securities and/or Sukuk Not Through a Public Offering brought private placements under the regulatory coverage of OJK. This regulation is also referred to as the private placement regulation and became effective on 1 June 2020.

The private placement regulation was not intended to impede private placement activities in the Indonesian bond market or change market practice; instead, OJK focused on creating legal certainty for issuing entities and investors by ensuring a regulatory basis for private placements as a form of issuance and formalizing a type of minimum disclosure obligation for greater transparency given regulatory trends in the region and elsewhere. This update note describes the resulting regulatory process for the issuance of debt securities and/or *sukuk* via a private placement.

Private placements need to (i) meet certain criteria for tenor and issuance value (see Chapter III.E for details), (ii) be issued in scripless form, and (iii) be deposited with KSEI. The number of investors into or holders of a private placement cannot exceed 49 during the tenure of the private placement.

A listing of a private placement on IDX is presently not possible (see also Chapter III.I for information on potential upcoming developments with regard to listing).

### a. Relevance of the Nature of the Entity Issuing a Private Placement

The private placement regulation also introduced a distinction of terms for entities aiming to issue a private placement, based on their nature and—chiefly—their ability to fulfill continuous disclosure obligations. While the terms used are not new—they are based on terminology employed in the Capital Market Law and previous OJK regulations and their official translations—their distinction appears in a regulation for the first time. The ASEAN+3 Bond Market Forum supports the taxonomy maintained by OJK and strives to use the terms as they were intended.

The English term "issuer" (Bahasa Indonesia: *emiten*) as used in law and regulations is associated with an entity issuing a public offering of (any) securities since the Capital Market Law was promulgated in 1995. The term "public company" refers to a company that, without having done a public offering, has at least 300 shareholders and paid-in capital of at least IDR3 billion, or such other number of shareholders and paid-in capital that may be stipulated in OJK regulations.

The term "offeror" (Bahasa Indonesia: *penerbit*) is used in the private placement regulation to represent the issuing entity of a private placement. The types of offeror in a private placement consist of (i) an issuer or a public company, (ii) a legal entity that is not an issuer or a public company, (iii) supranational institutions, and (iv) certain collective investment schemes (CIS). An offeror who does not presently have continuous disclosure obligations in the Indonesian market will have to obtain a credit rating, appoint an arranger to support its offering, and appoint a monitoring agent to review its activities and financial position throughout the lifecycle of the debt securities or *sukuk*. A nonresident entity who has not previously issued (any) securities in Indonesia or who does not have publicly offered debt securities outstanding will not be able to issue a private placement (see also section K in this chapter).

For the purpose of referencing distinctions between the different eligible entities issuing a private placement, this update note will classify the offerors of a private placement into those who have continuous disclosure obligations in the Indonesian market (issuers or public companies) and those who do not have such continuous disclosure obligations in the Indonesian market (not an issuer or a public company).

Figure 2.2: Regulatory Process Map—Private Placement Issuance in Indonesia

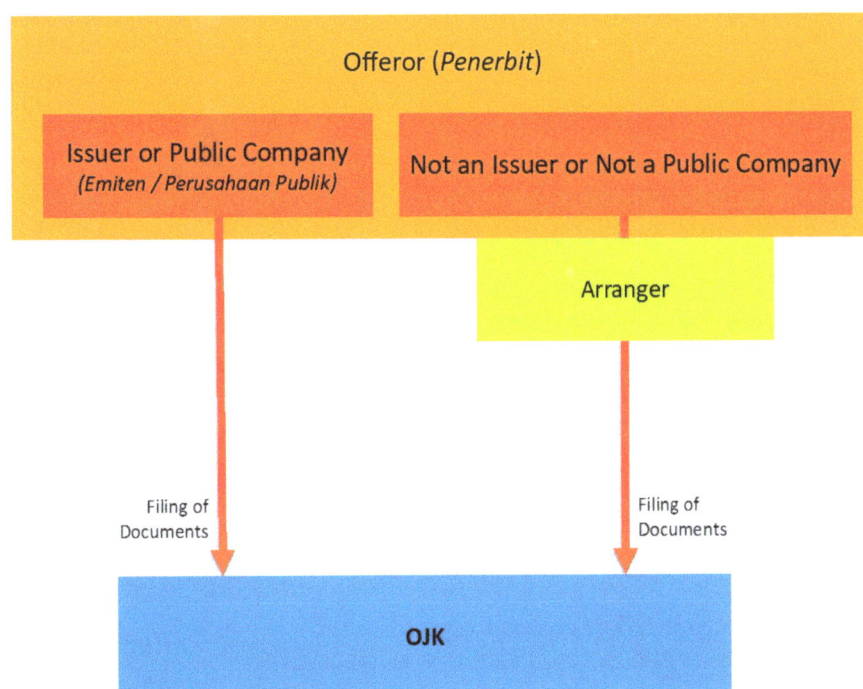

OJK = Otoritas Jasa Keuangan (Financial Services Authority).
Source: ASEAN+3 Bond Market Forum Sub-Forum 1 team.

The individual steps and requirements of the regulatory process for a private placement are detailed hereafter; the process reflects the concessions compared to the process for public offerings, as shown in section F.4 of Chapter II of the *ASEAN+3 Bond Market Guide for Indonesia* and in Figure 2.2 above.

### Step 1—Filing of Issuance Documentation with the Financial Services Authority

The entity planning to offer a private placement needs to file the issuance documentation with OJK prior to the issuance for the purpose of illustrating the necessary activities. If the approval of an industry regulator is required, such approval should be obtained prior to submitting issuance documentation to OJK.

Depending on the nature of the entity planning to offer the private placement, the issuance documentation will need to be submitted by the offeror itself or an arranger on behalf of an offeror. If an arranger is required or appointed, the arranger will have to be a securities company with an underwriting license granted by OJK. An offeror that is classified as an issuer or a public company submits its documents via SPRINT, while other types of offerors are presently required to have documents submitted to OJK in physical form or in electronic form via a data storage device.[13] The submission of information to OJK must be in Bahasa Indonesia; documents may be in more than one language as long as one of the languages is Bahasa Indonesia (see Chapter III.G for details). In practice, draft documents in English are often also submitted to OJK.

The provisions for issuance documentation and their contents are contained in Chapter VI of the private placement regulation. The key documents include a cover letter, the format of which is prescribed in the appendix of the private placement regulation and in the information memorandum.

The information memorandum is expected to contain all material information that investors are required to know to make an informed investment decision. The regulation prohibits the information memorandum from containing false or misleading information and requires the contents to be clear and well structured. Information must be provided in the order stipulated by the regulation and no sections may be skipped, even if they are not applicable to a particular issuance.

The components of the prescribed information (below) are further explained in individual articles of the private placement regulation and detailed hereafter. Market practice in the private placement market previously already included much of the information detailed here:

    i.     issue date or distribution date,
    ii.    a statement regarding the issuance,
    iii.   information regarding the offeror,
    iv.   information regarding the sponsoring company in the event that the offeror is a new legal entity formed by the sponsoring company,
    v.    information on the issuance,
    vi.   the use of proceeds,
    vii.   summary of important financial data,
   viii.   analysis and discussion by management,
    ix.   risk factors,
    x.    parties involved in the issuance, and
    xi.   procedures for subscribing to the private placement.

Specific statements regarding the issuance—such as identifying the issuance as a private placement—need to be placed prominently at the front of the information memorandum and provided in capital letters. The statements, here translated into English for convenience, need to read as follows:

> The Financial Services Authority Does Not Approve Or Agree To These Securities, Does Not Declare The Truth Or Adequacy Of The Content Of This Information Memorandum. Any Contradicting Statement Is Unlawful.

> The Offeror Is Fully Responsible For The Truth Of All Information, Facts, Data, Or Reports And Opinions Stated In This Information Memorandum.

> Issuance Of [These] Securities Is Not A Public Offering As Intended In The Capital Market Law And Issued Through A Private Placement Mechanism To Professional Investors.

> This Security Is Only For Sale To Professional Investors.

---

[13] While the submission of documents for issuances to professional investors does not yet occur via SPRINT, OJK envisages the acceptance of issuance documentation for public offerings of bonds or *sukuk* to professional investors and for private placements as a future development of SPRINT.

Information on the offeror of the private placement must contain the following details:

i. name, address, telephone, electronic mail address, and/or fax number;
ii. authorization and date of of establishment;
iii. main business activities currently being carried out, including a description of products and/or services offered, as well as business prospects;
iv. capital structure and ownership structure or its equivalent if the offeror is not a limited liability company;
v. major shareholders (if applicable);
vi. offeror business group information, if the offeror is part of a business group, which is made in the form of a structure;
vii. management and supervision arrangements; and
viii. the name of the party that can be contacted at the offeror.

Information on the sponsoring company needs to contain the following details:

i. name, address, telephone, electronic mail address, and/or fax number;
ii. main business activities currently being carried out;
iii. capital structure and ownership structure or its equivalent in the event that the sponsoring company is not a limited liability company;
iv. arrangement of management and supervision;
v. summary of important financial data for the last 3 years;
vi. analysis and discussion by management; and
vii. risk factors.

The required details on the issuance of the private placement need to include at least the following information:

i. type and maximum amount of issuance and number of issuances (if applicable);
ii. the transfer mechanism of the private placement and whether it can be traded;
iii. the book-entry unit and/or trading unit, including restrictions on book-entry, in the event that the private placement can be traded;
iv. summary of the rights of the holders of the private placement;
v. a summary of the nature of the private placement that allows for earlier payment of the choice of the offeror or holder of the private placement;
vi. requirements and/or restrictions on early payment of the private placement (if applicable);
vii. the bid (offering) price;
viii. interest rate, yield, or other means in the form of value or in the form of a range of interest rates, yields, or compensation by other means;
ix. date of payment of principal amount or principal amount due on that date;
x. the date of payment of interest, yield, or compensation by other means;
xi. for securities that can be converted into shares, including at least:
    a. a description of the terms of conversion including whether conversion rights will be lost if not exercised before the date disclosed in the repurchase announcement; and
    b. the start date and end date of conversion;
xii. summary of requirements regarding debt settlement funds in the event that there are requirements for debt settlement funds; and
xiii. the currency in which the private placement is denominated.

The offeror also needs to describe the reasons and procedures for holding a general meeting of bondholders, including provisions on attendance, quorum, and decision-making. Similarly, a description of instances of negligence that could lead to default and how such instances could be resolved will need to be included.

Should the private placement be rated, the rating information will need to be included, as would any approvals from a competent authority that the offeror required prior to filing issuance documents with OJK. If the private placement features a buyback option, provisions for the same need to be included.

Additional information is required if the issuance is guaranteed or secured. The offeror must also indicate any prohibitions or restrictions affecting the bondholders, and the offeror needs to declare any conflict of interest between itself and the parties involved in the issuance.

Should the offeror have outstanding debt securities, these need to be indicated in the information memorandum. In addition, the offeror will need to declare the seniority or primacy of the private placement in relation to existing debt securities and other potential liabilities that the offeror may acquire.

Information on the use of proceeds must include an estimation of the costs of the issuance to the offeror and be expressed as either a percentage of the issuance amount or an absolute value in the denomination currency.

The summary of important financial data is prescribed to include data at least for the last 2 financial years, or since the establishment of the offeror if the company has not yet been established for 2 years, as well as interim financial data if available. Financial data refer to a financial statement, a statement of profit or loss or other income statement, and significant ratios relevant for the industry of the offeror. Financial reports for the issuance need to be consistent in numbers and descriptions with those in the offeror's official financial report.

Management analysis and discussion information is expected to contain brief analysis of the financial reports and other information in the information memorandum, including the financial statement and income statement and applicable financial ratios. Risk factors need to describe material risk factors that could affect the offeror's condition.

The information memorandum also needs to include detailed information on the parties involved in the issuance:

    i.     their name, address, and description of the duties and responsibilities in the issuance; and
   ii.     details of their business registration and/or business activity license from OJK, as applicable.

Procedures for the subscription to the private placement must at least include the following information:

     i.     the offering period;
    ii.     the procedure for submitting a purchase order;
   iii.     the minimum quantity that can be ordered for each order;
   iv.     payment terms including confirmation of purchase and payment deadline;
    v.     electronic distribution; and
   vi.     registration with KSEI.

If the private placement is in the form of *sukuk*, the following additional information will need to be contained in the information memorandum:

    i.     a schedule or plan and procedures for the distribution and/or payment of profit sharing, margin, or service fee in accordance with the characteristics of the Sharia-compliant contract;

ii. confirmation that the assets that form the basis of the *sukuk* do not conflict with Sharia principles and the offeror guarantees that during its tenor the assets on which the *sukuk* is based will not conflict with Sharia principles;

iii. the types of Sharia-compliant contracts and transaction schemes as well as explanations of Sharia-compliant transaction schemes used in the issuance of the *sukuk*;

iv. a summary of the Sharia-compliant agreements made by the parties involved;

v. the source of income that becomes the basis for calculating the payment for profit sharing, margin, or service fee in accordance with the characteristics of the Sharia-compliant contract;

vi. the amount of the profit-sharing ratio, margin, or service fee in accordance with the characteristics of the Sharia-compliant contract;

vii. source of funds used to make payments for the results, margin, or service fee in accordance with the characteristics of the Sharia-compliant contract;

viii. replacement of the assets on which the *sukuk* is based if something happens that causes the value to no longer match the value of the *sukuk* issued, if and as necessary according to the characteristics of the Sharia-compliant contract;

ix. plans for the use of funds from the issuance of the *sukuk* in accordance with the characteristics of the Sharia-compliant agreements;

x. provisions for when the offeror fails to fulfill its obligations;

xi. the mechanism of handling situations should the offeror fail to fulfill its obligations;

xii. terms and conditions in case the offeror will change the type of Sharia-compliant contract, the content of the Sharia-compliant contract, and/or assets that form the basis of the *sukuk*;

xiii. a Sharia-compliant conformity statement for the *sukuk* from the National Sharia Board or a Sharia capital market expert; and

xiv. whether or not there is a deduction of *zakat* (charity) on the profit sharing, margin, or service fee, which is to be disclosed at the beginning of the offering information.

## Step 2—Actual Issuance

The private placement regulation does not require OJK to approve the issuance documentation, nor will OJK comment on the contents or information accuracy. However, OJK will check the completeness of information for compliance with the regulation.

The issuance of debt securities and/or *sukuk* must be carried out within 30 days after the issuance documentation has been filed with OJK.

In the event that an offeror makes changes to the issuance documentation prior to the actual issuance but after the filing of said documentation to OJK, a resubmission of all issuance documentation to OJK is required prior to the actual issuance. Noncompliance may attract administrative sanctions including warnings, fines, or suspension of business activities.

### 6.    Obligations after Approval and after Issuance

The requirement for the submission of application documents and statutory reporting via an electronic system is detailed here, as this is the section dedicated to reporting in this update note. Other sections containing the description of reporting obligations will make reference to this section for necessary details.

OJK Regulation No. 7/POJK.04/2018 on Submission of Reports via the Electronic Reporting System for Issuers or Public Companies was promulgated on 25 April 2018, requiring the submission by issuers of public offerings and public companies of reports prescribed in capital market regulations through the electronic system provided by OJK, called Reporting System for Issuers and Public Companies (SPE). The submission of reports through SPE became mandatory 6 months after the promulgation of OJK Regulation No. 7/POJK.04/2018, with issuers and public companies needing to obtain login details by that time. The regulation superseded previous OJK prescriptions on the electronic submission of reporting requirements.

It should be noted that SPE represents a different system with different underlying requirements than SPRINT (mentioned in section 4 of this chapter), which is used for the submission of Registration Statements and supporting documents prior to issuance as well as for listing applications to IDX.

OJK Regulation No. 7/POJK.04/2018 prescribes the use of SPE and its dedicated website for all reports to be submitted by issuers and public companies to OJK under capital market regulations, whether periodical or if requested by OJK; these include financial statements, material events, use-of-proceeds reports, sustainable finance reporting, bond issuance related announcements, and credit rating reports. The issuer or public company is deemed to have submitted a report through SPE if it has received an electronic receipt such as an email notification. Following the introduction of SPE, issuers and public companies did not need to continue submitting printed copies of reports or those via electronic storage media.

SPE is operated by IDX as a system provider on behalf of OJK and has been integrated with the IDXNet platform for disclosure information maintained by IDX (see also section J in this chapter for background information on this integration). The integration of the two systems (now known as SPE-IDXNet) allows an issuer or public company to submit relevant disclosure information or reporting once, with the system routing the document to the appropriate user.

Reporting deadlines, as well as form and contents of such reports, continue to follow the stipulations in the underlying capital market regulations for the type of reporting. Parties submitting reports still need to retain these reports in their own books and records according to applicable statutory retention periods, and data submitted via SPE must be the same as that in company records. Should discrepancies between the information submitted into SPE and the company records occur, SPE data would be treated as reference data.

The submission of reports via either SPE or an alternative method is detailed according to bond issuance types below.

### a.    Public Offerings

At the time of the compilation of this update note, the submission processes for public offerings and public companies were integrated through the electronic systems used by OJK and IDX.

#### To the Financial Services Authority

While the reporting requirements for public offerings have not changed, the submission of regulatory reporting by issuers of public offerings was changed in April 2018 to be via the dedicated OJK reporting portal, SPE (now SPE-IDXNet). Please see the lead-in text in this section for detailed information on SPE and the establishment of SPE-IDXNet. Following submission, OJK issues a confirmation of receipt via automatic email notification.

Reporting obligations for public offerings to professional investors are not yet submitted via SPE-IDXNet, with reporting continuing via physical submission or the submission of electronic copies on storage media directly to OJK.

### To the Indonesia Stock Exchange

Public companies and issuers of public offerings of debt securities that have been listed on IDX are able to submit their continuous disclosure information and relevant documents to IDX via IDXNet, which has since been integrated with SPE to form SPE-IDXNet. IDX issues a confirmation of receipt of documentation required under IDX rules via SPE-IDXNet as well as by automatic email notification.

### b.    Private Placements

Reporting requirements to OJK in relation to private placements were introduced following the effective date of the private placement regulation in June 2020 (see Chapter III.E for details on the regulation).

### To the Financial Services Authority

Offerors of private placements are required to submit the result of the issuance of a private placement to OJK. If the offeror is not an issuer, a public company, a certain type of CIS, or an entity issuing a private placement solely to limited-investment CIS, the report on the issuance result will need to be submitted by the arranger, otherwise the offeror may submit the report directly.

The report on the issuance result must be submitted in both hardcopy and electronic form, with the same information in both versions, and reach OJK no later than 5 working days after the issuance. The form and contents of the report are stipulated by OJK in the appendix to the private placement regulation. If OJK provides an electronic system for the submission of the issuance result, the report only needs to be submitted electronically.

In the case of a gradual issuance of the private placement, reports on the result of the issuance of individual tranches will need to be submitted within 5 working days after each tranche is issued.

At the time of the compilation of this update note, reports needed to still be submitted in hardcopy form and on electronic storage media directly to OJK.

### To Investors

Customized reporting obligations agreed between the offeror (as the case may be), capital-market-supporting institutions and professionals, and investors involved in a private placement need to be fulfilled on a contractual basis.

### 9.    Regulatory Process for Public Offerings to Professional Investors

OJK Regulation No. 11/POJK.04/2018 concerning Public Offering of Debt Securities and/or Sukuk to Professional Investors, referred to as the Public Offering to Professional Investors Regulation, became effective on 1 August 2018 and introduced the professional investors concept in the Indonesian bond market. In addition, the regulation enabled the additional issuance type of a public offering to professional investors.

The prescriptions for the new public offering type build on the general requirements for public offerings regulated in the Capital Market Law and subsidiary regulations, such as the submission of a Registration Statement and the use of a prospectus, their respective contents, the OJK regulatory process (see section 4 of this chapter for details) and other obligations, including disclosure, unless otherwise regulated in the professional investors regulation. As such, the professional investors regulation will have to be considered in conjunction with underlying prescriptions for public offerings in law and regulations.

While, for all intents and purposes, this issuance type represents a public offering to specific types of investors, the professional investors regulation does offer concessions to issuers compared with standard public offerings:

- the credit rating of the instrument is voluntary in principle but mandatory for multiple issuances under a shelf-registration (for the first issuance),
- audited financial statements need only be submitted for the last 2 financial years and may not need to be submitted for issuers (public companies) or those with debt securities outstanding,
- legal opinions required may cover fewer subjects, and
- selected sections in the prospectus may be omitted.

A listing of debt securities or *sukuk* publicly offered to professional investors remains at the discretion of the issuer (see also Chapter III.I for details on the listing process).

At present, reporting obligations for a public offering to professional investors set by OJK still require the submission of information in hardcopy form or via electronic copy on a storage media (see section 6 of this section for details).

## G.    Continuous Disclosure Requirements in the Indonesian Bond Market

### 1.    Where a Public Offering of Debt Securities Was Made

Continuous disclosure obligations for public offerings of debt securities or *sukuk* to professional investors follow the general continuous disclosure requirements for public offerings prescribed by OJK and IDX for listed debt securities and *sukuk*, respectively, as detailed in the *ASEAN+3 Bond Market Guide for Indonesia*.

As a result of the introduction of its electronic reporting system in 2018 (see section F.6 in this chapter), reporting obligations to OJK are to be submitted via SPE for standard public offerings instead of in hardcopy form or via electronic files as was described in the *ASEAN+3 Bond Market Guide for Indonesia*. Reporting for public offerings to professional investors continues to be carried out via hardcopy or electronic copies on storage media. Reporting deadlines and the form and contents of reports continue to follow the prescriptions in individual capital market regulations issued by OJK.

Pursuant to OJK regulations, IDX mandated the submission of disclosure information in electronic form via IDXNet; all disclosure documents prescribed in regulations and aimed at the public can be submitted via IDXNet. IDX issues a confirmation of receipt for documentation submitted via IDXNet and sends an automatic email notification, which is also received by OJK.

### 2.    Where a Private Placement Was Made

OJK Regulation No. 30/2018 introduced post-issuance and continuous reporting requirements in relation to private placements with effect from June 2020. The reporting requirements differ depending on the type of offeror (see section F.5 of this chapter or Chapter III.E for the distinction) and for market intermediaries in the secondary market.

Applicable reports for private placements are not yet to be submitted via SPRINT (see section F.6 of this chapter for details) but instead continue to be filed directly with OJK via hardcopy or in electronic format on storage media.

### a.    Private Placement by an Issuer or Public Company [NEW]

If the party carrying out the private placement is an issuer or public company (or a supranational institution or one of the eligible CIS), OJK does not impose any continuous disclosure requirements specific to the private placement. The issuer will still be subject to any continuous disclosure obligations stemming from its public issuances (see section 1 of this chapter), its underlying disclosure obligations (e.g., as a CIS), or those potentially agreed with the investors in the private placement.

If an issuer has obtained a credit rating for the private placement, the annual update of the credit rating follows the prescriptions in OJK Regulation No. 49/POJK04/2020 Regarding Rating of Debt Securities and/or Sukuk (see Chapter III.O for details).

### b.    Private Placement by an Offeror [NEW]

If the private placement was carried out by an offeror who is not an issuer or a public company, OJK requires the submission of a material information report by the monitoring agent or bond trustee (see Chapter III.M for details on this role) in the event of the following:

i.    if the offeror has been negligent or violated provisions in the issuance documentation; or
ii.    if evidence is received and generally accepted that the offeror can be deemed unable to carry out their obligations under the private placement, or the offeror is no longer able to manage or control most of its assets.

The offeror must also report to OJK any changes to the terms and conditions of the private placement. Any such changes must first be approved by the bondholders. The report to OJK is due within 5 working days after the bondholders' approval and needs to be submitted in hardcopy form or via electronic media.

The offeror or its arranger also has to report to OJK—again in hardcopy form or via electronic media—the result of the annual credit rating review, pursuant to provisions in OJK Regulation No. 49/2020 Regarding Rating of Debt Securities and/or Sukuk (please see Chapter III.O for details).

### c.    Market Intermediaries [NEW]

The private placement regulation requires securities companies that trade in private placements to report any such transactions to OJK by submitting a hardcopy report. At the same time, custodian banks carrying out the settlement and transfer of private placements in KSEI are required to submit details of these transactions to OJK; this is typically done by uploading transaction data into PLTE, the dedicated securities transaction reporting platform operated by IDX on behalf of OJK.

Additional requirements for continuous disclosure may be agreed between the offeror, market intermediaries, and investors; in such instances, additional requirements should be stated in the information memorandum for the private placement and need to be adhered to by the parties assuming any such commitment.

## J.    Indonesia Stock Exchange Rules Related to Listing, Disclosure, and Trading of Debt Securities

Since 2017, IDX has issued or amended listing and trading rules—affecting application and disclosure practices for bonds and *sukuk* listed on its market—as a result of the introduction of green bonds and *sukuk*, bond-related derivatives, the revision of OJK regulations, and as part of market-wide initiatives in response to the COVID-19 pandemic.

While IDX was licensed as a PPA for the Alternative Trading Platform (SPPA) and issued new regulations for trading, market conduct, and participants, these regulations are not covered in this section, as SPPA represents an organized trading platform for government and corporate bonds and *sukuk* in the OTC market. In addition, IDX did not act in its role as a market institution or SRO. Participation on SPPA is separate from that on the exchange market or any other trading platform currently in use. For detailed information on SPPA and the regulations issued for that marketplace, please refer to Chapter IV.B.6.

While the listing and disclosure rules of IDX have been amended, the IDX system used to receive and store listing applications and disclosure information has seen an integration with the respective systems of OJK. As a result, for example, the submission of a listing application to IDX and a Registration Statement for a public offering of debt securities to OJK can be done in one parallel submission to OJK and IDX.

### 1.    Debt Securities Listing Rules and Related Disclosure

In light of the strong growth and increasing breadth of Islamic finance instruments, IDX decided to distinguish between listing rules for debt instruments and those for *sukuk*. Details on the new or revised rules are provided in the following subsections.

#### a.    Rule Number I-B Concerning List of Debt Securities

IDX issued its Amendment to Rule Number I-B Concerning Listing of Debt Securities on 20 May 2020 to provide incentives for the listing of green bonds and *sukuk*, as well as the bonds and *sukuk* of small and medium-sized enterprises or municipal issuers. The amended rule supersedes a number of rules that had been in place since 2004 including IDX Decree SK-024/LGL/BES/XI/2004-I.F.1: Debt Securities Listing (for Listing Bonds and Sukuk), which had been referenced in the *ASEAN+3 Bond Market Guide for Indonesia*.

The purpose of the amendment was to bring the listing rule in line with recent OJK regulations introducing a more diversified issuer classification. The amendment also aligned the listing rule with the concept of electronic submission of the Registration Statement and supporting documents introduced by OJK not long prior. The draft listing rule amendment was approved by OJK on 3 March 2020.

In the listing rule amendment, incentives for regional (municipal) bonds and *sukuk* include a 50% discount on the annual listing fee in the official IDX fee schedule for a period of up to 5 years from the effective date of the amendment, as well as transitional arrangements for the submission of issuance documentation and continuous disclosure information via an electronic system (to be) provided by IDX. The amendment also sets new listing fees for corporate *sukuk* based on a scale of the nominal value of a *sukuk* issuance, recognizes multiple listings by the same issuer, and provides for a capped annual listing fee for issuances by small and medium-sized enterprises.

The amended listing rule also includes definitions for green bond and business activities considered green, pursuant to the OJK green bond regulations issued in 2017 (see Chapter III.B for details).

The text of the listing rule amendment is presently only available in Bahasa Indonesia.[14]

### b.    Rule Number I-E Concerning Obligation to Submit Information

IDX published the Amendment to Rule Number I-E Concerning Obligation to Submit Information (information disclosure rule) on 29 January 2021, with an effective date of 1 February 2021. The rule amendment had been approved by OJK on 22 December 2020. The amendment superseded the original Rule Number I-E (dating back to 2004) and selected provisions in other IDX rules. It also augmented the requirements detailed in IDX Circular Letter SE-00006/BEI/10-2019.

The purpose of the revision was to bring information disclosure for issuers or listed companies in line with a number of recent OJK regulations, specifically in relation to prescribed issuance documentation and the specified timelines for the submission of disclosure and reports. The rule also prescribed that financial statements are to be submitted in the Extensible Business Reporting Language (XBRL) format.[15]

Rule Number I-E is principally applicable to all issuers and listed companies, and it commits them to the submission of all disclosure information, documents, and reports required by OJK regulations and IDX rules in electronic form, using the IDXNet platform provided by IDX. IDXNet has since been integrated with SPE (see section F.6 in this chapter for details), with OJK appointing IDX as the system provider for the combined reporting system through the Chief Executive of Capital Market Supervisor Decision Number Kep-52/D.04/2019 Regarding Appointment of IDX as a System Provider of Electronic Reporting for Issuer and Public Companies.

The issuer or public company will at all times remain responsible for all of its information submitted and contained in the electronic reporting system, including the use and misuse of such information.

At present, the text of the information disclosure rule is available in Bahasa Indonesia only.[16]

---

[14] See https://www.idx.co.id/media/8680/peraturan_i_b_pencatatan_efek_bersifat_utang.pdf.
[15] The XBRL is the open international standard for digital business reporting managed by a global not-for-profit consortium, XBRL International. XBRL is typically used for the digital reporting of financial, performance, risk, and compliance information in financial and capital markets. For more information, please refer to https://www.xbrl.org.
[16] See https://www.idx.co.id/media/9622/peraturan_i_e_kewajiban_penyampaian_informasi.pdf.

c.    IDX Rule Number I-G Concerning Sukuk Listing [NEW]

IDX Rule Number I-G Concerning Sukuk Listing was published on 26 March 2021. The new rule was intended to further encourage the development of the *sukuk* market and recognized the need for special listing arrangements for *sukuk*. As such, the provisions for the listing of *sukuk* had been lifted from the general debt securities listing rules and given new form through IDX Rule Number I-G. The *sukuk* listing rule was also meant to align listing requirements with the relevant provisions on *sukuk* in OJK regulations such as Regulation No. 3/POJK.04/2021 Concerning the Implementation of Activities in the Capital Market.

IDX Rule Number I-G also contains listing fee concessions and transitional arrangements for the submission of issuance documentation and continuous disclosure information through electronic means first published in the Amendment to IDX Rule Number I-B in May 2020; the corresponding provisions in IDX Rule Number I-B have thus been revoked.

The text of the *sukuk* listing rule is presently only available in Bahasa Indonesia.[17]

## K.    Market Entry Requirements (Nonresidents)

The *ASEAN+3 Bond Market Guide for Indonesia* focused on the market entry requirements for nonresidents in relation to foreign exchange transactions and the Single Investor Identification (SID). The inclusion of the issuance of debt securities or *sukuk* via private placement under the remit of OJK resulted in a possible limitation for nonresident issuers, which is further explained in this section.

### 1.    Nonresident Entities

The promulgation of OJK Regulation No. 30/POJK.04/2019, effective in June 2020, also referred to as the private placement regulation, introduced distinctions between parties able to issue debt securities or *sukuk* via a private placement.

While these distinctions primarily center on an entity's ability to fulfill continuous disclosure obligations in the interest of investor protection, OJK clarified the application to these regulations for nonresident entities who had not previously issued debt securities or *sukuk* in Indonesia, or who do not have publicly offered debt securities outstanding at the time of a proposed issuance of a private placement.

According to OJK, a nonresident entity without ongoing continuous disclosure obligations in the bond market in Indonesia is not able to issue debt securities or *sukuk* via a private placement. However, the nonresident entity may issue debt securities or *sukuk* via a public offering. Such a public offering of debt securities or *sukuk* would also enable the nonresident entities (now classified as an issuer) to subsequently issue debt securities or *sukuk* via a private placement, as the public offering would have allowed OJK to assess disclosure and other information from the nonresident issuer.

---

[17] See https://www.idx.co.id/media/9739/peraturan_i_g_pencatatan_sukuk.pdf.

# III

# Characteristics of the Indonesian Bond Market

The introduction of a professional investors concept, the corresponding increase in issuance types, and the issuance of green bonds and green *sukuk* by both sovereign and corporate issuers—coupled with an overhaul of market regulations and rules— have changed or augmented the Indonesian bond market significantly since the publication of the *ASEAN+3 Bond Market Guide for Indonesia* in August 2017.

These changes to the Indonesian bond market's characteristics are described in this chapter in the context of the existing structure of the *ASEAN+3 Bond Market Guide for Indonesia*.

## A.    Definition of Securities

### 6.    Green Bond Definition in Financial Services Authority Regulations [NEW]

OJK Regulation No. 60/POJK/04/2017 on the Issuance and the Terms of Green Bond, issued in December 2017, defines green bonds as "bonds whose funds of proceeds are used to finance or refinance part or all of the activities of an environmentally sound business."

## B.    Types of Bonds, Notes, and Sukuk

The types of bonds, notes, and *sukuk* in the Indonesian market have expanded significantly since 2017 through an increase in number of green bond and green *sukuk* varieties, including savings and retail versions, endowment-linked *sukuk*, as well as sustainability bonds. Meanwhile, so-called "diaspora bonds" are in the planning stage. The new instrument types are described in this section within the structure used in the *ASEAN+3 Bond Market Guide for Indonesia*. Please also see Chapter I.E of the *National Strategy for Financial Market Development, 2018–2024*, which set many of the objectives leading to the new instruments.

IDX has also begun offering the trading of government bond-linked futures contracts; for more information on these instruments, please see Chapter IV.I.

### 1.    Debt Securities Issued by the Government

In addition to its range of debt instruments described in the *ASEAN+3 Bond Market Guide for Indonesia*, the Government of Indonesia now also issues green *sukuk* in a number of different variants. At the time of the publication of this update note, the Government of Indonesia had not issued sovereign green bonds.

To support the issuance of green *sukuk*, the Government of Indonesia released its *Green Bond and Green Sukuk Framework* in early 2018. The underlying assets for green *sukuk* are those eligible as green assets under the framework.

More detailed information on this government initiative and the *Green Bond and Green Sukuk Framework* are available from the website of the MOF.[18]

As the next stage, the Government of Indonesia has developed its *SDG Government Securities Framework*, a comprehensive framework that covers the various aspects of sustainable financing, including green, social, and also blue financing. The *SDG Government Securities Framework* will serve as guidance for sovereign issuances of green and blue and social and sustainability bonds and *sukuk* that will fund eligible projects delivering environmental and social benefits in line with the Indonesian 2030 development agenda. The framework and its Second Party Opinion from the Center for International Climate and Environmental Research–Oslo (CICERO) and the International Institute for Sustainable Development were published in September 2021.

### m.    Government Green Sukuk [NEW]

The MOF issued the first green *sukuk* on 1 March 2018, following the establishment of the Government of Indonesia's *Green Bond and Green Sukuk Framework* (see also Chapter X.A). The government received a second opinion and assurance on the framework from CICERO on 23 January 2018.

This first green *sukuk* had an issuance volume of IDR16.75 trillion (USD1.25 billion at the time), with all proceeds going exclusively to eligible green projects based on the *Green Bond and Green Sukuk Framework*. The *sukuk* was issued under an existing global *sukuk* program, in the form of *wakalah* trust certificates, with a profit rate of 3.75% and a tenor of 3 years. The *sukuk* carried a second-party opinion from CICERO to ensure adherence the *Green Bond and Green Sukuk Framework* and the underlying Green Bond Principles.

Details on the issuance, the allocation of proceeds, and other salient subjects can be found in *Indonesia's Green Bond and Green Sukuk Initiative*, a report prepared by the United Nations Development Programme.[19]

Just like other sovereign *sukuk*, green *sukuk* issuance follows Law Number 19 of 2008 Concerning Government Sharia Securities; green *sukuk* represent a different type of *sukuk*, not an instrument of a different nature. When announcing the proposed issuance volume of sovereign bonds and *sukuk*, the MOF will detail the planned issuance amount and type of *sukuk*, now including green *sukuk*.

The Government of Indonesia has continued issuing green *sukuk* every year since the original green *sukuk* issuance in 2018.

### n.    Government Retail Green Sukuk–Savings Sukuk (Sukuk Ritel–Sukuk Tabungan) [NEW]

The Government of Indonesia issued its first green savings *sukuk* in November 2019, raising IDR1.46 trillion.[20] The issuance of this savings *sukuk*, referred to as Series ST006 and interchangeably as retail green *sukuk*, represented the first global retail green *sukuk*. Like the original retail and savings *sukuk* issued by the government, the green *sukuk* was issued to Indonesian citizens only, this time via authorized distributors including fintech

---

[18] See https://www.djppr.kemenkeu.go.id/uploads/files/dmodata/in/6Publikasi/Offering%20Circular/ROI %20Green%20Bond%20and%20Green%20Sukuk%20Framework.pdf.
[19] See https://www.undp.org›dam›docs›pubs-reports.
[20] The press release is available in Bahasa Indonesia on the MOF website at https://www.djppr.kemenkeu.go.id/page/load/2673.

companies, as well as the e-SBN online platform (see also section E in this chapter).

ST006 was issued in a denomination of IDR1 million with a tenor of 2 years. Each retail investor could purchase up to IDR3 billion of the green savings *sukuk*. The floating interest rate was linked to the official BI 7-day reverse repo rate, with a floor of 5.0%. Rewards from profit sharing are payable quarterly. Like the original savings *sukuk*, the green savings *sukuk* are nontradable and come with the option of early redemption. The Sharia principle underlying the green savings *sukuk* is *wakalah*.

A Series ST007 of the green savings *sukuk* with the same characteristics was issued on 20 November 2020, again via authorized distributors and e-SBN.

### o.    Cash Waqf-Linked Sukuk (Endowment-Linked Sukuk) [NEW]

Cash *waqf*-linked *sukuk* (CWLS) are Islamic bonds or *sukuk* linked to endowments (*waqf*). CWLS allow investors with a SID and a securities account to buy *sukuk* that deliver coupons (hence, the mention of cash), as a type of donation, to organizations that administer endowment funds (e.g., social and welfare projects such as health care, education, and poverty alleviation). The proceeds from CWLS are allocated to the state budget. Investors in CWLS receive back their principal investment upon maturity or have the option to assign the principal to the endowment organizations at that time.

Endowment-linked *sukuk*—also transliterated into Bahasa Indonesia as *sukuk wakaf*—may be offered in variants for institutional investors and for retail investors (*sukuk wakaf ritel*) and issuance size may depend on the type and number of endowments that are linked. CWLS are nontradable, with a fixed coupon to generate expected contributions, and do not feature specific denominations, owing to the nature of the instrument. The tenor of issued CWLS has ranged from about 2 years to about 4 years.

The first CWLS was issued on 10 March 2020. At the time of writing, the Government of Indonesia had issued three series of CWLS via a variation of private placements and by using online and offline book-building exercises. CWLS issuances are designated as SW999, while retail CWLS are designated as SWR999; the underlying Sharia principle used is *wakalah*.

So far, the Government of Indonesia has issued only IDR-denominated CWLS, but it has not ruled out issuing CWLS in other currencies in the future. While CWLS are part of the Surat Berharga Syariah Negara (government *sukuk*) category that can be issued in either Indonesian rupiah or a foreign currency, the MOF also must observe Government Regulation Number 42 of 2008, which stipulates that CWLS must be denominated in rupiah, while CWLS issued in a foreign currency should be converted to rupiah. However, this regulation is in the process of revision.

For more details on the nature and purpose of CWLS, please refer to Chapter VIII of this update note.

### p.    Diaspora Bonds (Considered) [NEW]

The MOF has been studying the introduction of a bond type aimed at Indonesian citizens living abroad since 2019. The approach is based on the likely investment potential from overseas Indonesians and the ability to distribute electronic retail bond and *sukuk* issuances via the successful e-SBN portal (see also section E in this chapter). The MOF is exploring options for issuances in both Indonesian rupiah and US dollars, and will also consider the readiness of potential distribution partners and platforms.

An investor would have to meet specific criteria to be eligible to invest in this bond. The MOF is working with the Ministry of Foreign Affairs to set such eligibility criteria and observe any investment restrictions that may apply in other markets with regard to overseas assets.

While the term "diaspora bond" is being considered, an official name for this bond type has not yet been formally determined.

### 4.    Bonds, Notes, and Sukuk Issued by the Corporate Sector

Corporates and financial services institutions have been issuing green bonds in the Indonesian market since 2018 and sustainability bonds since 2019. At present, following the promulgation of the OJK Regulation on the Issuance and the Terms of Green Bond and the OJK Regulation on Private Placement, green and sustainability bonds may be issued via a public offering or via private placement (see also section E in this chapter).

To be able to issue green and sustainability bonds, corporate issuers or offerors will have to comply with regulations and publish a green and/or sustainability bond framework in which they explain their internal processes to identify, finance, and assess eligible projects and track the use of proceeds.

OJK has set itself the target to develop a green taxonomy in 2021–2022 by establishing a clear set of guidelines on what constitutes green assets.

### d.    Green Bonds [NEW]

The issuance of green bonds by corporates was facilitated by OJK Regulation No. 60 (POJK/04/2017) on the Issuance and the Terms of Green Bond, promulgated on 21 December 2017. The regulation referenced the International Capital Market Association's (ICMA) Green Bond Principles, contained a definition of green bond (see section A in this chapter) and the criteria for eligible business activities, and focused on the additional application and disclosure practices required for green bonds on the basis of existing requirements for a public offering of debt securities and applicable disclosure obligations. Green and sustainability bonds may be issued in Indonesian rupiah or foreign currency.

Pursuant to the regulation, a green bond will require the use of a minimum of 70% of its proceeds to finance business activities and/or other activities aimed at protecting, restoring, and/or improving the quality or function of the environment. The issuer or offeror would also be required to buy back the bonds should the green credentials used to substantiate the green bond issuance no longer be valid.

The regulated specific activities eligible for the green bond label include

- renewable energy;
- energy efficiency;
- pollution prevention and control;
- natural resource management and sustainable land use;
- biodiversity conservation;
- environmentally friendly transportation;

- sustainable water and wastewater management;
- climate change adaptation;
- eco-efficient products;
- environmentally friendly buildings that meet national, regional, or international standards or certification; and
- other activities that are environmentally friendly or have environmental benefits.

The issuer or offeror of green bonds will need to maintain a separate account for the green bond proceeds, or provide separate account notes in its financial statement, and submit regular reports on the performance of the underlying green projects to OJK.

The first issuance of a corporate green bond was conducted in July 2018 by PT Sarana Multi Infrastruktur, a state-owned infrastructure finance company. Its green bonds were issued in the amount of IDR500 billion in two tranches of 3-year and 5-year bonds under a shelf-registration, with 100% of the proceeds dedicated to eligible business activities.

### e. Sustainability Bonds [NEW]

Sustainability bonds finance projects for green and/or social initiatives.

In the absence of OJK regulations specific to sustainability bonds (an existing OJK regulation is specific to green bonds issued via a public offering), corporate issuers or offerors can still issue sustainability bonds via private placement and align their sustainability bond framework with international sustainability bond principles, as was the case of the sustainability bonds issued by Bank Rakyat Indonesia (BRI) and Bank Mandiri (see below). For the private placement of a sustainability bond, corporate offerors still have to comply with the existing OJK regulation to the extent relevant.

BRI issued the first sustainability bond by a financial services institution in March 2019, with the proceeds going to the financing of social and environmental projects. The bond issuance volume was USD500 million, and it had a tenor of 5 years.

Prior to the issuance, BRI had published its BRI Sustainability Bond Framework, which is aligned with the ICMA's Sustainability Bond Guidelines, Green Bond Principles, and Social Bond Principles; the framework also conforms to the ASEAN Sustainability Bond Standards set by the ASEAN Capital Markets Forum.

Bank Mandiri issued its first sustainability bond in April 2021, following the publication of its sustainability bond framework in early 2021, which also built on the prescriptions in international and ASEAN standards. The issuance raised USD300 million for a 5-year tenor and proceeds were to be allocated to projects with an environmental or social focus. The third-party opinion for the referenced sustainability bonds was provided by Sustainalytics.[21]

More information on the sustainability bond frameworks and issuances are available from the websites of the respective companies or from the reports of the Climate Bonds Initiative (see link in Appendix 2).[22]

---

[21] Adapted by the ASEAN+3 Bond Market Forum Sub-Forum 1 team from available information in the public domain.
[22] For Bank Mandiri, see https://www.bankmandiri.co.id/documents/38265486/0/Sustainability+Framework+-+Sustainability+Bond+Bank+Mandiri+2021.pdf/81c20119-c4de-06fe-e419-8e32b3468967. For BRI, see https://www.ir-bri.com/misc/SR/BRI-Sustainability-Framework-Final-March-vF.pdf.

## E.    Methods of Issuing Bonds and Notes (Primary Market)

This section details changes or additions to issuance methods and issuance types, and the emergence of new issuance channels in the Indonesian bond market, following the structure of the *ASEAN+3 Bond Market Guide for Indonesia*.

### 1.    Government Securities

While the Government of Indonesia has introduced new debt instruments since 2017, such as variants of green *sukuk*, the corresponding issuance methods have not changed with one notable exception, the increasing use of the electronic issuance platform for retail and savings *sukuk*, e-SBN.

### e.    Issuance via e-SBN [NEW]

e-SBN is the electronic issuance and distribution platform for retail and savings government securities (conventional and *sukuk*) issued by the Government of Indonesia. e-SBN was launched in 2018 and is owned and operated by the MOF. Appointed banks, securities firms, and fintech companies—acting as selling agents—offer access to e-SBN via their own online platforms. Since 2019, sales of retail government securities have been conducted exclusively via e-SBN.

Online distribution of sovereign issuances via e-SBN is aimed at domestic investors, particularly to increase the participation of millennials or younger investors in savings instruments, and follows the key goal of the government to further financial inclusion. A review of Indonesian retail *sukuk* investment undertaken by the MOF had previously revealed that after 10 years of retail *sukuk* issuance, around 75% of investors were aged 40 years or above.[23] Following the introduction and active use of e-SBN, about 70% of investors were reported to be aged 30 years or below. e-SBN was also able to reach investors in more remote locations without the presence of securities firms or selling agents.

e-SBN was established in 2018 as a digital distribution channel through MOF Regulation Number 31 of 2018 (PMK 31/2018) and was affirmed through MOF Regulation Number 27 of 2020 Concerning the Sale of Retail Government Securities (PMK 27/2020). The MOF regulation is available for download in Bahasa Indonesia from the MOF website.[24]

In contrast to the quota system previously used, e-SBN offers all investors equal access, with a current minimum order size of IDR1 million (and a maximum of IDR3 billion), and the option of an early redemption for nontradable instruments. Tradable retail government securities cannot be traded or transferred via e-SBN in the secondary market. The first instrument to be issued through e-SBN was retail conventional bond series SBR003.

MOF provides the ability for banks, securities firms, and fintech companies to participate in the distribution by providing access to e-SBN via their websites or online platforms, with OJK assessing and regulating these entities and their capabilities, including on cybersecurity.

e-SBN allows a retail investor to set up an online account and subscribe to new retail issuances via the platform; for the typical terms of the retail government

---

[23] The press release from the MOF about the review is available only in Bahasa Indonesia at https://mediakeuangan.kemenkeu.go.id/Home/Detail/77/e-sbn-mudahkan-investasi.
[24] See https://jdih.kemenkeu.go.id/FullText/2020/27~PMK.08~2020Per.pdf.

securities, please see section B.1.n in this chapter. The investor must be an Indonesian citizen and will need a SID generated by KSEI, a bank account, and a securities account to hold the retail government securities. Banks and securities firms or fintech firms integrate the e-SBN portal into their online services and branding, offering payment options for settlement of the subscription order (from investor accounts or via third parties), subscription status and history, portfolio viewing, early redemption, and other facilities.

The e-SBN website is maintained in Bahasa Indonesia only.[25]

### 3.    Bonds and Notes Issued by the Private Sector (Corporate Bonds)

A regulation prescribing the introduction of the professional investors concept, as well as the private placement regulation issued by OJK, created an additional or amended existing issuance method for bonds and *sukuk* in the Indonesian bond market. In addition, the ability to issue securities via crowdfunding platforms added a new issuance method to the market, which has also become available for debt securities.

### a.    Public Offering

Regulations issued by OJK since the publication of the *ASEAN+3 Bond Market Guide for Indonesia* did not change the issuance method of a public offering but adjusted or clarified parts of the application and issuance process, and added the variant of a public offering to professional investors (see section e in this chapter). The relevant changes are described in Chapter II.F.4 and other sections.

### c.    Private Placement

The Capital Market Law has recognized the issuance of debt securities or *sukuk* via private placement since its inception in 1995. With effect from 1 June 2020, OJK Regulation No. 30/POJK.04/2019 Concerning Issuance of Debt Securities and/or Sukuk Not Through a Public Offering, also referred to as the "private placement regulation," formally integrated private placements into the regulatory framework for the bond market in Indonesia. The intention of the new regulation was not to create new rules but to bring legal and regulatory certainty to issuing entities and investors for a market segment that had evolved on the basis of market practices alone.

As such, the issuance of a private placement does not require an approval from OJK, but the new regulation stipulates minimum disclosure standards and distinguishes between qualifications of the parties undertaking the issuance, in particular with regard to experience in information disclosure. Please see also Chapter II.F.5 for a comprehensive description of the regulatory process for private placements. Private placements may be issued via a single or continuous offerings (see also the next section).

The original characteristics of a private placement remain valid. A private placement is defined as an offer of securities to a maximum of 100 parties with purchase by no more than 49 buyers. No official marketing or offer material may be made available except to the intended maximum number of investors. No advertising, public communications (print, TV, and online ads), or general marketing may be undertaken. Should any of the above stipulations be breached, the bond or *sukuk* issue in question will automatically be considered a public offering and be subject to all applicable regulations as well as approval by OJK.

---

[25] See https://www.kemenkeu.go.id/sukuktabungan.

In addition, the private placement regulation prescribes that only professional investors may invest in private placements, and they have to establish their credentials to the issuing entity (see below) or arranger at the time of purchase (see also section N in this chapter for details on the professional investors concept).

Through the private placement regulation, OJK introduced the distinction of terms in Bahasa Indonesia, and the corresponding terms in English translations of the regulation, for the entities planning to issue debt securities via private placement. These terms follow and expand on the formal definitions in law and other regulations and have significance for eligibility to issue, credit rating, and the need to appoint market intermediaries such as an arranger and monitoring agent or trustee.

While the English term "issuer" is well established in the international context as a party issuing (debt) securities, the use of *emiten* in the Indonesian market only represents an entity having issued a public offering that is still outstanding and, as a result, subject to disclosure obligations. Public companies are also already subject to continuous disclosure obligations. Other entities considered similar to an issuer are supranational institutions and eligible CIS, all of which are subject to their own disclosure obligations.

In contrast, the English term "offeror" (in Bahasa: *penerbit*) applies in the context of a private placement to the issuing entity. Offerors may be (i) an issuer or a public company, (ii) a legal entity that is not an issuer or a public company, (iii) supranational institutions, and (iv) certain CIS. Among such offerors, there are those who do not have current disclosure obligations and are thus subject to additional requirements and scrutiny.

Depending on the nature of the entity wishing to issue a private placement, a private placement may need to be rated (see section O.3 in this chapter for details on credit rating requirements for private placements). A credit rating may be replaced with a guarantee for the private placement or with insurance coverage for the issuance; in both cases, the guaranteed or insured value must be at least 100% of the nominal value of the issuance.

Debt securities or *sukuk* issued via a private placement have to be deposited with KSEI and need to follow prescriptions for minimum issuance size and denomination. The private placement regulation also places the responsibility for the information disclosure on the issuing entity and prescribes the minimum contents of the information memorandum that has traditionally been used as the key disclosure document for private placements.

The information memorandum needs to be submitted to OJK in Bahasa Indonesia, but depending on the target investor universe, it may also be produced in English. Issuers and public companies are required to produce disclosure information in their annual reports and on their websites in Bahasa Indonesia as well as in a foreign language(s) that includes, at least, English.

Presently, private placements are not eligible for listing on IDX. However, with private placements under the regulatory remit of OJK since June 2020, and newly defined disclosure and other requirements aimed at aiding investor protection, there is market expectation that this status might be reviewed in the future.

### d.    Note Issuance Programs (Gradual Issuance)

The private placement regulation contains provisions for the continuous or gradual issuance of debt securities or *sukuk* via private placements. While there is no specific mention of a note issuance program, or even the term program, the features prescribed in the regulation are comparable to a note issuance program as practiced in other markets.

Gradual issuance (the regulation refers to "issuance in stages") must be completed within a 2-year period and there are no limitations to the number of tranches that may be issued in that period. If a credit rating is obtained, it will need to apply to the entire planned issuance amount at the time of the first issuance. The initial information memorandum will need to prominently identify the issuance method as gradual and contain the planned total amount of issuance.

For each subsequent tranche, a supplementary information memorandum needs to be filed with OJK at least 1 day prior to issuance. Such a supplementary information memorandum needs to make reference to the original filing of the gradual issuance with OJK and contain the issuance amount of the respective tranche, credit rating or change of credit rating from previous tranches issued (if so applicable), a summary of important financial data based on the latest available financial statements, and any additional relevant information or changes to information in the information memorandum of the first or previous issuance, among other details. The other prescriptions for a private placement (see section c in this chapter) also apply.

The use of gradual issuance via private placement is expected to address the practice of reverse enquiry that has been popular with issuing entities and investment managers in the Indonesian bond market.

### e.    Public Offering to Professional Investors [NEW]

The issuance of corporate bonds or *sukuk* via a public offering was supplemented with the option to issue via a public offering to professional investors only, following the introduction of the professional investors concept in OJK Regulation No. 11/POJK.04/2018 Concerning Public Offering of Debt Securities and/or Sukuk to Professional Investors. The regulation became effective on 1 August 2018.

A public offering to professional investors follows the principal prescriptions for a public offering and requires the compilation of a prospectus, the submission of a Registration Statement, as well as approval from OJK. Unlike other public offerings where the submission of Registration Statements and supporting documentation is made via SPRINT, the submission of the Registration Statement and supporting documentation to OJK for a public offering to professional investors is not yet facilitated via SPRINT (details in Chapter II.F.6).

At the same time, this issuance method allows for concessions for the issuer, recognizing that professional investors are able to better analyze relevant information on the issuance. These concessions extend to a credit rating not being mandatory (other than for continuous offerings), a reduction of the number of years of financial data to be provided, the coverage of fewer subjects in required legal opinions, and the ability to omit certain sections of the prospectus. Please see Chapter II.F for details on the differentiation of the regulatory processes between public offerings and those to professional investors only.

Public offerings to professional investors can only be sold to professional investors that have proven their credentials to the issuer, arranger, or appointed securities companies prior to issuance. Please see section N in this chapter for a complete description of professional investor types and their eligibility criteria.

### f.    Crowdfunding of Debt Securities [NEW]

To support the funding avenues of start-up and small and medium-sized enterprises, OJK enabled the crowdfunding of securities through regulations in 2018 and expanded the crowdfunding scope to debt securities and/or *sukuk* via OJK Regulation No. 57/POJK.04/2020 Concerning Offering of Securities through Crowdfunding Services Based on Information Technology in December 2020; the regulation was further updated via POJK No. 16/POJK.04/2021 in August 2021.

The issuance of debt securities or *sukuk* via crowdfunding is not considered a public offering, hence, the entity issuing the debt securities or *sukuk* is referred to as *penerbit* (offeror) instead of *emiten* (issuer); please see Chapter II.F.5.a for a detailed explanation of the use of and distinction between these terms. Issuance via crowdfunding is also subject to specific requirements: (i) instruments need to have a tenor of less than 2 years and must be issued in Indonesian rupiah only; (ii) the issuance must be completed within 12 months; and (iii) during that period, a maximum of IDR10 billion can be raised.

The proceeds from the crowdfunding need to be allocated to a specific project for which the funding is sought. Crowdfunding organizers need to be either a limited liability company or a cooperative for services. Specific eligibility criteria for the organizer exist in terms of minimum capital and ownership.

Crowdfunding is carried out via a crowdfunding platform that is operated by a crowdfunding organizer, which must obtain a business license from OJK and prove the technological and operational capabilities of its crowdfunding platform prior to obtaining such a license. Once the crowdfunding organizer is licensed, it can facilitate the issuance of securities via the platform without offerors needing to file documentation for individual issuances with OJK.

At the same time, the crowdfunding organizer will need to ensure that the offerors and their issuances comply with the requirements set out in OJK Regulation No. 57/POJK.04/2020 (later updated to POJK No. 16/POJK.04/2021); this includes the need to review the offeror's legal status and the to-be-funded projects and issuance documentation, as well as ensuring prescribed continuous disclosure from the offeror throughout the tenor of the crowdfunded securities. Another obligation of the crowdfunding organizer is to ensure that investors meet the requirements of the regulation and only eligible investors can invest via the crowdfunding platform. The regulation requires the crowdfunding organizer to provide periodical reports to OJK.

The crowdfunding organizer will also have to establish a process for the deposit of the crowdfunded securities with KSEI through custodian banks for participants to open securities accounts for its investors. As of June 2021, KSEI had established cooperation with three crowdfunding platforms.

## G.    Language of Documentation and Disclosure Items

The information provided here on language of documentation and disclosure items in the Indonesian market supplements or adjusts previous statements in the same section in the *ASEAN+3 Bond Market Guide for Indonesia*, in recognition of the increase in interest in the use of language in ASEAN+3 professional bond markets.

### 1.    Legal Basis

Indonesia passed Law No. 24 of 2009 on National Flag, Language, Emblem and Anthem, typically referred to as the Language Law or Flag Law, effective 9 July 2009. Article 31 of the law made it mandatory that any contract or agreement involving an Indonesian private entity would have to be drawn up and executed in Bahasa Indonesia. As a result, any agreement with an Indonesian private entity not in Bahasa Indonesia would run contrary to the law and be considered as prohibited. Making the prescription for language mandatory in the law also precludes the possibility of any implementing regulation reducing or removing such prescription.

Litigation in relation to a loan agreement not in Bahasa Indonesia but signed after Law No. 24 of 2009 was promulgated became a test court case in this regard. In 2015, the Supreme Court of the Republic of Indonesia affirmed the previous decisions by a district court and a high court (on appeal) that the loan agreement contravened the law. This effectively means that a legal agreement with an Indonesian entity without including a Bahasa Indonesia version is null and void. This was further reaffirmed in Presidential Regulation Number 63 of 2019 Concerning the Use of Indonesian Language (PR 63 of 2019). This presidential regulation obliges all parties to use the Indonesian language when they enter into an agreement.

OJK strives to make the requirements in relation to language of documentation and disclosure easier by including specific prescriptions in new or amended regulations.

### 2.    Documentation in Regulatory Processes

A Registration Statement for a public offering, including for a public offering to professional investors, and any supporting documents, will need to be submitted to OJK in Bahasa Indonesia pursuant to Bapepam-LK Rule IX.A.1, which was published in 2011 and remains in force.

Similarly, the information memorandum for a private placement, as well as its supporting documents, will need to be submitted to OJK in Bahasa Indonesia. Supporting documents may be in a language other than Bahasa Indonesia, if accompanied by a translation into Bahasa Indonesia by a sworn translator. In practice, the original version of the documents that are written in languages other than Bahasa Indonesia will likely also be submitted to OJK.

An information memorandum may be published in English if agreed between parties involved in a private placement (e.g., for the purpose of attracting foreign institutional investors). However, such an English version would not fulfill the prescriptions of the private placement regulation, and a version of the information memorandum in Bahasa Indonesia would have to be submitted to OJK. The submission of issuance documentation in two languages (e.g., as a bilingual version) is acceptable as long as one of them is Bahasa Indonesia.

### 3.    Language for Correspondence [NEW]

OJK will declare a Registration Statement effective in a letter or email (depending on the medium through which the Registration Statement was received by OJK) in

Bahasa Indonesia, and issue any other correspondence in relation to regulatory processes in Bahasa Indonesia. If the issuing entity is a nonresident entity, the correspondence made by OJK in the process of reviewing the Registration Statement and the notification letter of the effectiveness of the Registration Statement issued by OJK will be presented in Bahasa Indonesia. In addition to the Bahasa Indonesia version, where possible, the correspondence and effective letter may also be presented in English. In case of inconsistencies and differences in interpretation, the Bahasa Indonesia version shall prevail.

Pursuant to the original Bapepam Rule II.A.3 promulgated in 1997 and never revoked, letters, reports, applications, and other documents that are submitted to Bapepam (now OJK) must be in Bahasa Indonesia. Documents in a foreign language must be translated into Bahasa Indonesia, except for documents referred to in Rule IX.A.8 Regarding Preliminary Prospectuses and Information Memoranda. The OJK website carries the full text of Bapepam Rule II.A.3.[26]

### 4. Language in Relation to Disclosure [NEW]

IDX requires the submission of documents as well as disclosure information in Bahasa Indonesia; if an issuer or offeror submits bilingual information, one of the languages must be Bahasa Indonesia.

OJK Regulation No. 8/POJK.04/2015 Regarding Website of Issuers or Public Companies prescribes that issuers of public offerings of debt securities—or public companies—shall present their website in Bahasa Indonesia as well as in foreign language(s), which must include English. In addition, OJK Regulation No. 29/POJK.04/2016 Regarding Annual Report of Issuers or Public Companies prescribes that all annual reports need to be published in Bahasa Indonesia as well as in foreign language(s), which must include English.

### 5. Other Market Documentation [NEW]

KSEI accepts supporting documents (e.g., business registration certificate or similar document) for the opening of an account on behalf of a foreign institutional investor in English, where the document itself is presented in English. Applications to KSEI for a SID for nonresident investors are processed via an online application with screens and field names in English; text in free format fields is accepted in English.

Custodian banks servicing nonresident investors can present agreements, account opening forms, and terms and conditions in more than one language (i.e., in Bahasa Indonesia and in English). For purposes such as client onboarding and the establishment of tax status, constitutional documents of nonresident investors (e.g., articles of association and business register excerpts) are accepted in in English only.

In relation to tax processing or a tax reclaim, nonresident investors are required to submit a certificate of residence in English; the form stipulated by the Directorate General of Taxation (DGT) to establish a nonresident investor's tax status is in English, pursuant to DGT regulations.

---

[26] See https://www.ojk.go.id/en/kanal/pasar-modal/regulasi/klasifikasi-bapepam/dokumen-publik-dan-laporan/Pages/ii-a-3-letters-reports-and-other-documents-that-are-sent-to-bapepam.aspx.

## H.    Registration of Debt Securities

The basic concept of the registration of debt securities and the other meanings of the term registration used in the Indonesian bond market are explained in Chapter III.H of the *ASEAN+3 Bond Market Guide for Indonesia*. However, the need or the ability to register debt securities was expanded through regulations that have come into force more recently, specifically regulations on public offerings to professional investors, private placements, and crowdfunding of debt securities.

### 6.    Public Offerings to Professional Investors [NEW]

Implemented on 1 August 2018, the additional issuance method of public offerings to professional investors gives prospective issuers some concessions with regard to credit rating and details of disclosure information. As for any public offering, the issuer will need to submit to OJK a Registration Statement and supporting documents. However, in contrast to other public offerings, the Registration Statement as well as supporting documents are not yet to be submitted through SPRINT; the submission still needs to be made in physical form and in electronic form via a data storage device.

The public offering to professional investors as an issuance method is described in detail in section E.3 of this chapter.

### 7.    Private Placements [NEW]

With the introduction of OJK Regulation No. 30/2019 (see Chapter II.F for details), which became effective on 1 June 2020, issuances of debt securities or *sukuk* via a private placement must be registered with OJK. While the submission of a Registration Statement is not required, the issuer or offeror or their arranger will need to file issuance documentation pursuant to the prescriptions in the regulation, in effect registering the private placement with OJK. As of the time of writing, the filing does not yet occur via SPRINT.

In addition, the private placement regulation makes it mandatory for privately placed debt securities or *sukuk* to be registered at and deposited with KSEI; this was previously a voluntary activity. Pursuant to the private placement regulation issued by OJK, KSEI amended its Regulation Number II-B Regarding Registration of Debt Securities and/or Sukuk at KSEI with effect from 15 October 2020. The KSEI regulations are available in English from its website.[27]

Further details on private placement as an issuance method are provided in section E.3 of this chapter. The regulatory process for a private placement is described in detail in Chapter II.F.5 in this update note.

### 8.    Crowdfunded Debt Securities [NEW]

Pursuant to OJK Regulations on Offering of Securities through Crowdfunding Services Based on Information Technology (POJK No. 57/POJK.04/2020, later updated to POJK No. 16/POJK.04/2021), offerors of debt securities issued via electronic crowdfunding platforms have the ability to register at and deposit crowdfunded securities with KSEI (or a custodian).

Please also see section E.3 in this chapter for further information on the issuance of securities via crowdfunding platforms.

---

[27] KSEI regulations are typically available in English at https://www.ksei.co.id/files/translation_Peraturan _KSEI_Nomor_II-B_tentang_Pendaftaran_EBU_upload.pdf.

## I.    Listing of Debt Securities

The basis and regulatory process for a listing of debt securities on IDX has not changed since the publication of the *ASEAN+3 Bond Market Guide for Indonesia*. However, IDX moved to adjust its listing rules in response to new issuance and instrument types to bring disclosure obligations, concessions, and practices in line with the prescriptions in applicable OJK regulations and to allow for electronic submission of disclosure information. Please see Chapter II.J in this update note for a review of the listing rule changes and their drivers.

At the end of July 2021, IDX reported 51 new listings of corporate bonds and *sukuk* since the beginning of the year, bringing the total number of listings of corporate bonds and *sukuk* to 468 from a total of 126 listed issuers. The outstanding nominal value for 2021 listings amounted to IDR54.03 billion and the total outstanding nominal value of listed corporate bonds and *sukuk* reached IDR424.12 trillion and USD47.5 million for those instruments listed in US dollar. Government debt securities listed on IDX numbered 139 series, with a nominal value of IDR4,287.15 trillion and USD400 million for USD-listed instruments. In addition, 11 asset-backed securities were listed, totalling IDR6.20 trillion

This section briefly reviews the new instrument and issuance types eligible for listing in the context of the structure used in the *ASEAN+3 Bond Market Guide for Indonesia*.

### 1.    Public Offerings

In addition to debt securities and *sukuk* issued via public offerings, IDX now also admits debt securities and *sukuk* issued via a public offering to professional investors. The Professional Investors Regulation (OJK Regulation No. 11/POJK.04/2018) itself does not contain references to a listing but identifies other regulations covering public offerings as also being relevant for a public offering to professional investors in terms of disclosure obligations and other prescriptions. This includes that a listing remains at the discretion of the issuer; if so selected, the listing intention will need to be included in the issuance documentation, including in the Registration Statement.

In this context, Article 76 of the Capital Market Law stipulates that in the event a Registration Statement states that securities are to be listed on an exchange but listing requirements are not met, the public offering of such securities shall be null and void, and subscription moneys shall be returned to subscribers.

Effective 20 May 2020, IDX also added the ability for green bonds and *sukuk*, municipal and regional bonds and *sukuk*, and bonds and *sukuk* of small and medium-sized enterprises to list on its main board.[28] These bonds and *sukuk* can take advantage of a more favorable listing fee structure. All of these bonds and *sukuk* will need to be issued via either a public offering or a public offering to professional investors to be eligible for listing; the listing rules stipulate any specific characteristics expected of each type of bond or *sukuk* (e.g. green bonds).

The first corporate green bond was issued by PT Sarana Multi Infrastruktur, a state-owned infrastructure finance company, and listed on IDX on 10 July 2018.

While the listing process for public offerings to professional investors follows the established process for public offerings, the ability for the issuer of a public offering to professional investors to not obtain a credit rating (unless the offering is continuous),

---

[28] The IDX announcement of the listing eligibility for the new instruments is available from the IDX website, presently only in Bahasa Indonesia, at https://idx.co.id/media/8651/peraturan_i_b_pencatatan_efek_bersifat_utang.pdf.

as well as other concessions in relation to initial disclosure, have been recognized by IDX in its most recent revisions of the listing rules. Rating requirements will no longer apply if the underlying OJK regulation does not prescribe a rating as mandatory.

The promulgation of a dedicated listing rule for *sukuk* in March 2021 (see Chapter II.J.1.c for details) has made the listing process and underlying eligibility and listing characteristics distinct from the established process for conventional debt securities. However, for all intents and purposes, the process described in the *ASEAN+3 Bond Market Guide for Indonesia* remains otherwise valid.

### 3.    Private Placements

IDX presently only governs the listing of debt securities issued via a public offering.

It is presently envisaged that, going forward, issued bonds, whether listed or unlisted, including those issued via private placement, may be voluntarily listed on an Alternative Trading Platform.

## K.    Bond and Note Pricing

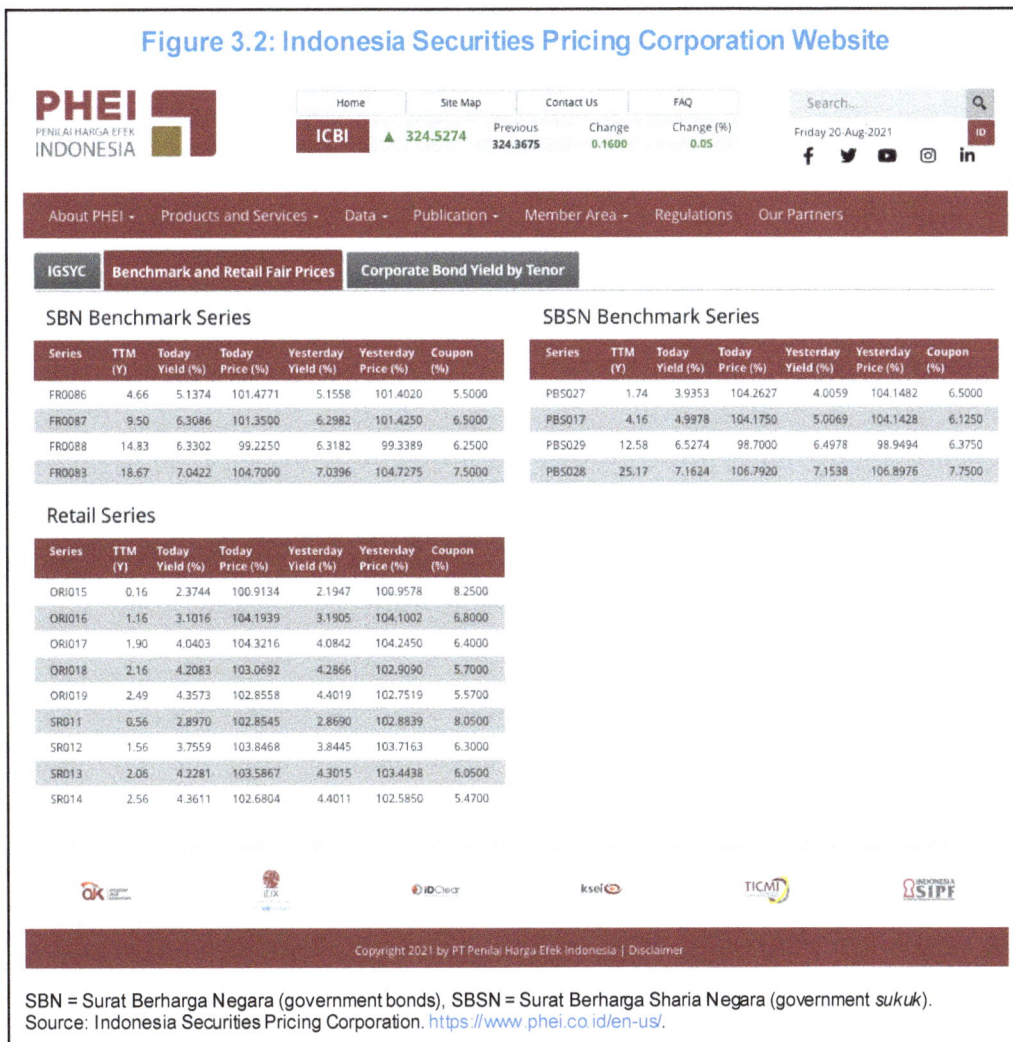

### Figure 3.2: Indonesia Securities Pricing Corporation Website

SBN = Surat Berharga Negara (government bonds), SBSN = Surat Berharga Sharia Negara (government *sukuk*).
Source: Indonesia Securities Pricing Corporation. https://www.phei.co.id/en-us/.

In 2019, the Indonesia Bond Pricing Agency (IBPA) changed its branding in English to the Indonesia Securities Pricing Corporation. Its new acronym, PHEI, reflected its name in Bahasa Indonesia, Penilai Harga Efek Indonesia. PHEI maintains its website in Bahasa Indonesia and English and offers a synopsis of its data on a microsite exclusively in English (see Chapter IV). Figure 3.2 provides an image of the new website's appearance.

PHEI continues to offer reference pricing of debt securities issued in the Indonesian market, regardless of whether these are traded OTC, on the exchange, or in organized markets such as SPPA (see Chapter IV for details).

## M.    Market Participants

### 3.    Parties Involved in Debt Securities Issuance

#### f.    Trust Agent (Bond or Sukuk Trustee)

Through OJK Regulation No. 19/POJK.04/2020 Concerning Commercial Banks Conducting Activities as Trustees, promulgated on 23 April 2020, OJK sought to consolidate provisions for and strengthen the capabillities, independence, and professionalism of the trustee function carried out by commercial banks. The function of the trustee itself remained unchanged.

The regulation prescribes the need to get a license from OJK for trustee activities upon meeting detailed requirements and sets out the main duties and responsibilities, obligations, and prohibitions of a commercial bank acting as trustee. Under the regulations, the trustee license may be cancelled upon violation of these obligations or when a commercial bank no longer fulfills the requirements stated in the regulation.

#### j.    Arranger [NEW]

An arranger is not a new type of participant in the Indonesian bond market but rather a role specifically designated in the private placement regulation promulgated by OJK in 2019 and effective 1 June 2020.

The appointment of an arranger is required for entities wishing to issue a private placement but without having current continuous disclosure obligations; the arranger is expected to guide such an offeror (see section E.3 in this chapter for details on the terminology) through the raising and filing of issuance and disclosure documentation with OJK. An arranger will need to be a securities firm that has obtained an underwriting license from OJK.

#### k.    Monitoring Agent [NEW]

The introduction of the private placement regulation (see also section E in this chapter) prescribed the appointment of a so-called monitoring agent (Bahasa Indonesia: *agen permantau*) by an entity planning to issue debt securities or *sukuk* via a private offering that is not an issuer, a public company, a certain type of CIS, or other entity issuing a private placement to limited investment CIS. Please see section E.3 in this chapter for more details on the terminology used.

The function of the monitoring agent is similar in nature to the trust agent or bond trustee (see section M.3.f in the *ASEAN+3 Bond Market Guide for Indonesia* and the update above); in fact, a monitoring agent has to have a trust agent license from OJK (see above) and is, typically, a bank. However, the prescriptions for the need to appoint a monitoring agent, as well as the roles of such a monitoring agent for private placements, are sufficiently specific that the function is being separately listed here.

Under the private placement regulation, the monitoring agent is required to review the regular business activities of an offeror and to keep itself appraised of the offeror's financial situation. The monitoring agent needs to report to OJK any of the following events:

i.   if the offeror has been negligent or violated provisions in the issuance documentation, or
ii.  if evidence is received and generally accepted that the offeror can be deemed unable to carry out their obligations under the private placement, or the offeror is no longer able to manage or control most of its assets.

A monitoring agent is also required if an issuer or a public company offering debt securities through a private placement ceases to be an issuer or public company before the maturity date of the debt securities or *sukuk*.

## N.   Definition of Professional Investors

The Capital Market Law does not contain a professional investors concept. In light of a regional trend toward the ring-fencing of professional bond markets and after extensive study and consultations, OJK introduced regulations containing a formal definition for professional investors, effective 1 August 2018, which also introduced the issuance of a public offering aimed at such professional investors while granting issuers corresponding concessions (see section E in this chapter).

### 1.   Professional Investors [NEW]

OJK promulgated OJK Regulation No. 11/POJK.04/2018 Concerning Public Offering of Debt Securities and/or Sukuk to Professional Investors, with effect from 1 August 2018, which introduced the formal definition of professional investors, their categories, and applicable eligibility criteria. This update note will reference OJK Regulation No. 11/POJK.04/2018 as the Public Offering to Professional Investors Regulation since it contains both issuance type and professional investor provisions.

The professional investors definition is divided into financial services institutions and parties other than financial services institutions. Among the financial services institutions, banks and insurance companies are also further detailed according to common distinctions in the Indonesian market. The eligibility of parties other than financial services institutions is linked to certain eligibility criteria according to capabilities, investment experience, and net assets.

Professional investors include the following:

*Financial services institutions*

i.   banks, which consist of
   -   commercial banks,
   -   Islamic commercial banks, and
   -   branch offices of banks domiciled abroad;
ii.  pension funds;
iii. insurance companies, which consist of
   -   insurance companies,
   -   Sharia-compliant insurance companies,

- reinsurance companies, and
- Sharia-compliant reinsurance companies;

iv. investment managers, including investment products that are managed and/or the customers they represent; and

v. securities companies.

*Parties other than financial services institutions*

These parties need to have the ability to buy securities, have investment experience in the capital market for at least 1 year, and carry out risk analysis on investments in these securities. Classified into individuals or legal entities, they must meet the following eligibility criteria:

i. individuals with

- net assets of at least IDR10 billion (excluding land, buildings, and intangible assets); or
- an average capital market investment portfolio of at least IDR3 billion in 1 year prior to, and net of, the issuance of a public offering of debt securities and/or *sukuk* to professional investors;

ii. legal entity, joint venture, association, or organized group with

- net assets of at least IDR20 billion excluding land, buildings, and intangible assets; or
- an average capital market investment portfolio of at least IDR6 billion in 1 year prior to, and net of, the issuance of a public offering of debt securities and/or *sukuk* to professional investors.

Individuals and corporates may prove their experience in the capital market with ownership of a securities account, as evidenced through a statement of ownership or most recent audited financial statement, respectively. Individuals and corporates may also substitute the proof of their ability to conduct risk analysis on investments in securities with the use of investor advisory services.

Professional investors need to prove their eligibility to the issuer or offeror or underwriter (in the primary market) and the securities company or custodian bank (in the secondary market). Please also see details on transfer and selling restrictions in section Q in this chapter.

## O.    Credit Rating Requirements

This section covers the applicable credit rating requirements for debt securities and *sukuk* issued in the Indonesian bond market. For details on the underlying regulations on credit rating agencies and their business, which remain in force, please refer to Chapter II.N in the *ASEAN+3 Bond Market Guide for Indonesia*.

The credit rating requirements for the issuance of debt securities and/or *sukuk* in the Indonesian market have undergone substantial adjustments and additions since the publication of the *ASEAN+3 Bond Market Guide for Indonesia*. In late 2020, OJK replaced the original rules on credit rating stemming from Bapepam and Bapepam-LK supervision with a dedicated OJK regulation. In the 2 years prior, OJK had issued regulations for public offerings to professional investors as well as for private placements; both regulations also contained provisions for the treatment of credit ratings specific to each of these new issuance types.

### 1.    Credit Rating Requirements for Public Offerings

Effective 11 December 2020, the Minister of Law and Human Rights of the Republic of Indonesia promulgated OJK Regulation No. 49/POJK.04/2020 on Credit Rating of Debt Securities and/or Sukuk. The regulation replaced Bapepam Rule IX.C.11 and Bapepam-LK Decree Kep-712/BL/2012 and its attachments, and clarified and expanded the credit rating prescriptions to include issuances using a shelf-registration.

The credit rating provisions in this regulation apply to all debt securities or *sukuk* issued through a public offering with a maturity of more than 1 year at the time of issuance. The issuer will need to obtain a credit rating for each of the debt securities or *sukuk* issued and publish such rating in the prospectus, as well as include the credit rating in the trust agreement between trust agent and issuer. If the issuer decides to obtain more than one credit rating, all such credit ratings will have to be shown in the issuance documentation accordingly. Credit ratings may only be issued by a credit rating agency licensed by OJK.

The credit rating information for particular debt securities and/or *sukuk* will need to contain specific information on the issuer (e.g., prospects of the issuer and risk factors for the investors), be expressed as a credit rating symbol, and include the validity period of such rating (i.e., within 12 months from the date the rating was published). The period between the publication of the credit rating and the effective date of the registration statement (see also Chapter II.F) may not exceed 6 months.

On an ongoing basis, until maturity and repayment of the debt securities or *sukuk*, the issuer is required to disclose a credit rating update no later than 10 working days after the expiry date of an existing credit rating. If the issuer had appointed more than one credit rating agency (CRA) at the time of issuance, only one CRA may produce annual updates of the credit rating. If the rating update is different from the previous credit rating, the issuer is required to make an announcement no later than 10 working days after the expiry date of the existing credit rating, stating the details of and reasons for the change. The announcement has to be submitted to OJK via SPE in addition to any public announcement.

Should the rating change come as a result of a material event, the issuer must notify OJK via SPE and announce this connection to a material event to the public no later than 2 working days after the change is known to the issuer and state the relevant reasons. These actions are required for every credit rating attached to the debt securities or *sukuk* in case there are multiple ratings with changes.

Listed issuers need to announce obtaining a credit rating or a change in credit rating on their website and the IDX disclosure website, while nonlisted issuers must make such announcements on their website and in at least one national newspaper stipulated by OJK (see also Chapter III.G for continuous disclosure obligations). Proof of newspaper announcement must be submitted to OJK via SPE no later than 2 working days after the announcement date.

If an issuer wishes to pursue a gradual issuance of debt securities or *sukuk* using a shelf-registration, the credit rating at the time of the first issuance will need to cover the entire planned issuance amount of the debt securities or *sukuk*. Changes to credit ratings over the tenure of a gradual issuance will need to be applied to the entire issuance amount of the debt securities or *sukuk*.

## 2. Credit Rating Requirements for Public Offerings to Professional Investors [NEW]

Through OJK Regulation No. 11/POJK.04/2018 concerning Public Offering of Debt Securities and/or Sukuk to Professional Investors, OJK introduced a professional investors concept as well as concessions related to credit ratings for this new issuance type.

In contrast to public offerings to all investors, an issuer of a public offering of debt securities and/or *sukuk* to professional investors does not need to obtain a credit rating unless such public offering is intended to be issued in stages via gradual issuance (see also section 1 in this chapter). However, an issuer of a public offering to professional investors may choose to obtain a credit rating voluntarily, for example, to cater to specific types of institutional investors that can only invest in rated instruments.

If a credit rating is obtained, information on the credit rating will have to be included in the Registration Statement for the public offering to professional investors to be submitted to OJK, and a rating update will need to be submitted to OJK on an annual basis. The submission of a credit rating update occurs via SPE.

## 3. Credit Rating Requirements for Private Placements [NEW]

With the promulgation of OJK Regulation No. 30/POJK/04/2019, effective 1 June 2020, OJK brought private placements in the Indonesian bond market under its regulatory coverage. The regulation also defined credit rating requirements for private placements.

The need to obtain a credit rating depends on the party issuing the debt securities or *sukuk* via a private placement, hereby referred to as an offeror. (Please also see section E in this chapter for clarification on the use of specific terms for different parties issuing debt securities via private placement.)

An offeror of a private placement must obtain a credit rating for a private placement if it is not an issuer (of a previous public offering) or a public company, while an issuer or a public company may choose to obtain a rating. The credit rating needs to be issued by a CRA licensed by OJK. If the offeror is a supranational institution, the credit rating can be issued by an international CRA. The credit rating should have been issued no longer than 1 year prior to the time of the filing of complete issuance documents with OJK.

If an offeror wants to issue a private placement in stages (also referred to as gradual issuance in the regulation) and the private placement needs to or is intended to be rated, the credit rating must cover the planned issuance amount over the entire period of issuance.

## Q. Market Features for Investor Protection

As reported in the *ASEAN+3 Bond Market Guide for Indonesia*, OJK had recognized the need to offer issuers of debt securities and/or *sukuk* additional avenues of fundraising and had studied various ways to help support the growth of the Indonesian capital market without compromising investor protection mechanisms. The outcome included the introduction of a professional investors concept and the coverage of private placements under the OJK regulatory umbrella.

### 9. Introduction of Professional Investors Concept [NEW]

OJK introduced the professional investors concept in 2018, following substantial research on professional investor regimes in regional markets and the consideration of eligibility criteria appropriate for the Indonesian capital market.

#### a. Professional Investors Concept

The professional investors concept identifies financial services institutions—such as banks and securities companies, insurance companies, and pension funds—as well as eligible corporates and high-net-worth individuals as professional investors. Please see section N in this chapter for a comprehensive review of the investor types and eligibility criteria for professional investors.

#### b. Selling and Transfer Restrictions

The professional investors concept is applicable to both public offerings of debt securities and/or *sukuk* aimed at professional investors and private placements and features strong selling and transfer restrictions, holding responsible the issuer or offeror and/or market intermediaries—underwriter, securities companies, and custodian banks—for the adherence to these restrictions.

At the time of issuance and sale of debt securities and/or *sukuk* aimed at professional investors in the primary market, professional investors must declare to the issuer, offeror or underwriter, as the case may be, that they meet the professional investors eligibility criteria in a written statement that is part of the sales documentation.

In the secondary market, securities companies who help professional investors buy debt securities and/or sukuk aimed at professional investors must satisfy themselves that the buyers qualify as professional investors, while both securities companies and custodian banks need to ensure they only process the receipt of such debt securities for professional investors in their clients' securities accounts at KSEI. Securities companies and custodians are required to refuse purchase or settlement instructions for such debt securities if the buyers are not professional investors.

### 10. Introduction of Regulation for Private Placements [NEW]

With the introduction of OJK Regulation No. 30 (POJK/04/2019) on the Issuance of Debt Securities and/or Sukuk Not Through a Public Offering—also referred to as the private placement regulation—the issuance of private placements of debt securities and/or *sukuk* came under the purview of OJK. Effective 1 June 2020, entities wishing to issue private placements—terminology does play an important role in this regard—need to register their private placements with OJK and adhere to a number of prescriptions, specific eligibility for concessions, or the appointment of intermediaries or service providers.

To ensure maximum investor protection, while granting concessions on issuance approval and disclosure practices, private placements may only be sold to professional investors. For that purpose, the private placement regulation referenced the professional investors concept established in OJK Regulation No. 30/2018 and its selling and transfer restrictions (see description in previous section).

The private placement regulation also prescribes the need to appoint a monitoring agent, equivalent to a bond or *sukuk* trustee (see section M in this chapter for details) for entities wishing to issue debt securities or *sukuk* that do not have other formal disclosure obligations in the Indonesian capital markets at the time of issuance, such as public companies or issuers of publicly issued debt securities still outstanding. The monitoring agent acts as a safeguard to identify financial or other challenges outside of normal disclosure channels.

The process of issuing private placements and applicable provisions for different types of issuing entities are described in detail in Chapter II.F.5.

# IV

# Bond and Note Transactions and Trading Market Infrastructure

Information in this chapter relates to developments in bond market trading, transactions, and related subjects that have occurred since the publication of the *ASEAN+3 Bond Market Guide for Indonesia* and is presented in the context of the structure used in that bond market guide.

## A. Trading of Bonds, Notes, and Sukuk

Debt instruments issued in the Indonesian market may be traded on exchange or in the OTC market, including on the SPPA introduced in November 2020.

## B. Trading Platforms

In late 2020, the SPPA offered by IDX was added to the range of secondary trading platforms available in the Indonesian bond market. SPPA marks an addition to existing international and in-house OTC bond trading platforms of market participants that were described in the *ASEAN+3 Bond Market Guide for Indonesia*. Detailed information on SPPA is provided in section 6 below.

### 6. Alternative Trading Platforms [NEW]

On 9 November 2020, IDX launched SPPA, a new electronic trading platform that allows the trading of government and corporate bonds and *sukuk*. SPPA represents an extension of the proposed OTC trading platform, previously designated as ETP, and follows extensive development of the platform under the project name ETP Phase 2; however, SPPA represents an entirely new system. Please see Chapter IV.B.5 in the *ASEAN+3 Bond Market Guide for Indonesia* for the origins of ETP.

SPPA does not represent a new market segment on exchange, but rather it is an organized OTC trading platform for bonds and *sukuk* in the secondary market. The ability to establish SPPA is based on OJK Regulation No. 8/POJK.04/2019 Concerning Alternative Market Organizers, promulgated in February 2019, with the term "alternative" indicating a formal trading venue other than an exchange. The regulation requires the Alternative Market Organizer (PPA) to ensure a fair and efficient market operation, pursuant to prescriptions in the Capital Market Law and implementing regulations. The regulation requires that a PPA issues market rules to govern an Alternative Market Platform.

IDX had already previously been licensed though OJK Letter Number 46/KDK.01/2016 Concerning License as Organizer of Government Debt Securities Trading, pursuant to Bapepam Rule III.D.1 Concerning Organizer of Government Debt Securities Trading, based on its experience in establishing and managing organized markets for securities trading. While Rule III.D was subsequently replaced by OJK Regulation

No. 8/POJK.04/2019, parties with a license under the old rule did not need to apply for a new license as a PPA.

The introduction of SPPA followed detailed consultations with primary dealers and other stakeholders in the Indonesian bond market and was aimed at increasing liquidity and efficiency in the government bond market. SPPA was developed in conjunction with AxeTrading.

Trading on SPPA is open to financial market institutions only, and SPPA participants are considered separate from exchange members or the participants of other trading platforms. As of 11 June 2021, IDX had admitted 28 trading participants to SPPA. IDX is in discussions with Bloomberg on whether Bloomberg users may be allowed to access SPPA in the future; at the time of compilation of this update note, Bloomberg was still in the process of assessing the technical specifications for SPPA.

Trades agreed through SPPA can be settled directly between participants through KSEI, as is the current practice in the OTC bond market. At the same time, IDX is exploring the possibility of conducting a clearing and settlement facility through IDClear.

In its capacity as Alternative Market Organizer for SPPA, IDX issued a number of market rules for the new marketplace on 9 November 2020:

   i.    Rule on Determination of Tradable Securities through SPPA,
   ii.   SPPA Securities Trading Rules,
   iii.  SPPA Service User Rules, and
   iv.   SPPA Trade Control Rules.

The Rule on Determination of Tradable Securities through SPPA states that securities eligible for trading on SPPA include debt securities and *sukuk* issued via a public offering, government securities, and any other debt securities and *sukuk* as may be determined by OJK, as is prescribed in OJK Regulation No. 8/POJK.04/2019. At the time of the compilation of this update note, OJK had not yet determined any further debt securities and *sukuk* for trading on SPPA. Hence, the potential exists for OJK to include debt securities and *sukuk* issued not through a public offering (private placements) as eligible securities for trading on SPPA in the future.

IDX subsequently issued Circular Letter Number SE-00004/BEI/01-2021 on 21 January 2021 on Parameters of Trading in Debt Securities and Sukuk in the Alternative Trading Platform, which contained information on price quotation, minimum trading volume, tick sizes, and settlement cycles for specific instrument categories. The provisions became effective on 8 February 2021. The circular letter is presently only available in Bahasa Indonesia.[29]

The current list of trading participants is shown on the IDX website.[30] Regulations issued for SPPA by IDX as Alternative Market Organizer may be accessed via the list of Directives issued by IDX Directors;[31] they are only available in Bahasa Indonesia but are marked as relating to SPPA in the list.

---

[29] See https://www.idx.co.id/media/9579/se_00004_bei_01_2021_parameter_perdagangan_sppa.pdf.
[30] See https://www.idx.co.id/en-us/members-participants/list-of-indonesia-alternative-market-trading-system-user/.
[31] See https://www.idx.co.id/peraturan/keputusan-direksi.

## C.  Mandatory Trade Reporting

### 1.  Transactions Included in Trade Reporting

The mandatory trade reporting for transactions in the secondary market now includes private placements.

The private placement regulation issued by OJK in 2019 and effective since June 2020 prescribes that securities companies or custodians carrying out trades or settlement transactions in private placements are required to report such transactions to OJK. The reporting requirements and frequency follow separate OJK regulations on securities transaction reporting. Market parties typically input or upload their transaction data into PLTE, the transaction reporting platform operated by IDX on behalf of OJK.

### 2.  Reporting from SPPA into PLTE [NEW]

SPPA, established and operated by IDX, is the first formal OTC market segment in the Indonesian bond market (see also section B.6 in this chapter). Trades executed on SPPA are reported into the PLTE System on a real-time basis. In contrast, trades concluded in the OTC market directly between counterparties need to be entered into the PLTE System by the trading counterparties.

## F.  Yields, Yield Curves, and Bond Indices

In 2019, IBPA—then known as the Indonesia Bond Pricing Agency—changed its branding to the Bahasa Indonesia name of *Penilai Harga Efek Indonesia* (PHEI), which translates into English as the Indonesia Securities Pricing Corporation. Following a transition period for the purpose of name recognition for its previous work, where PHEI maintained IBPA as a website handle that linked to the website in Bahasa Indonesia, PHEI will only maintain the website under its new name going forward.[32] The full website is also available in English.[33]

### 1.  Yields and Yield Curves for Government and Corporate Bonds

PHEI maintains a microsite in English that serves as dashboard for all relevant information on bond trading activities (Figure 4.5). The information on the microsite includes yield-by-tenor tables for both government bonds and corporate bonds, PHEI's own yield curves for Indonesian government securities, and aggregate and individual yield curves by domestic credit rating categories. The microsite also offers the download of PHEI reports in English that were released in the past 4 weeks.

At present, the trade data and related information on the PHEI website does not include trades executed on SPPA.

---

[32] See https://www.phei.co.id.
[33] See https://www.phei.co.id/en-us/.

### Figure 4.5: Indonesia Securities Pricing Corporation Microsite

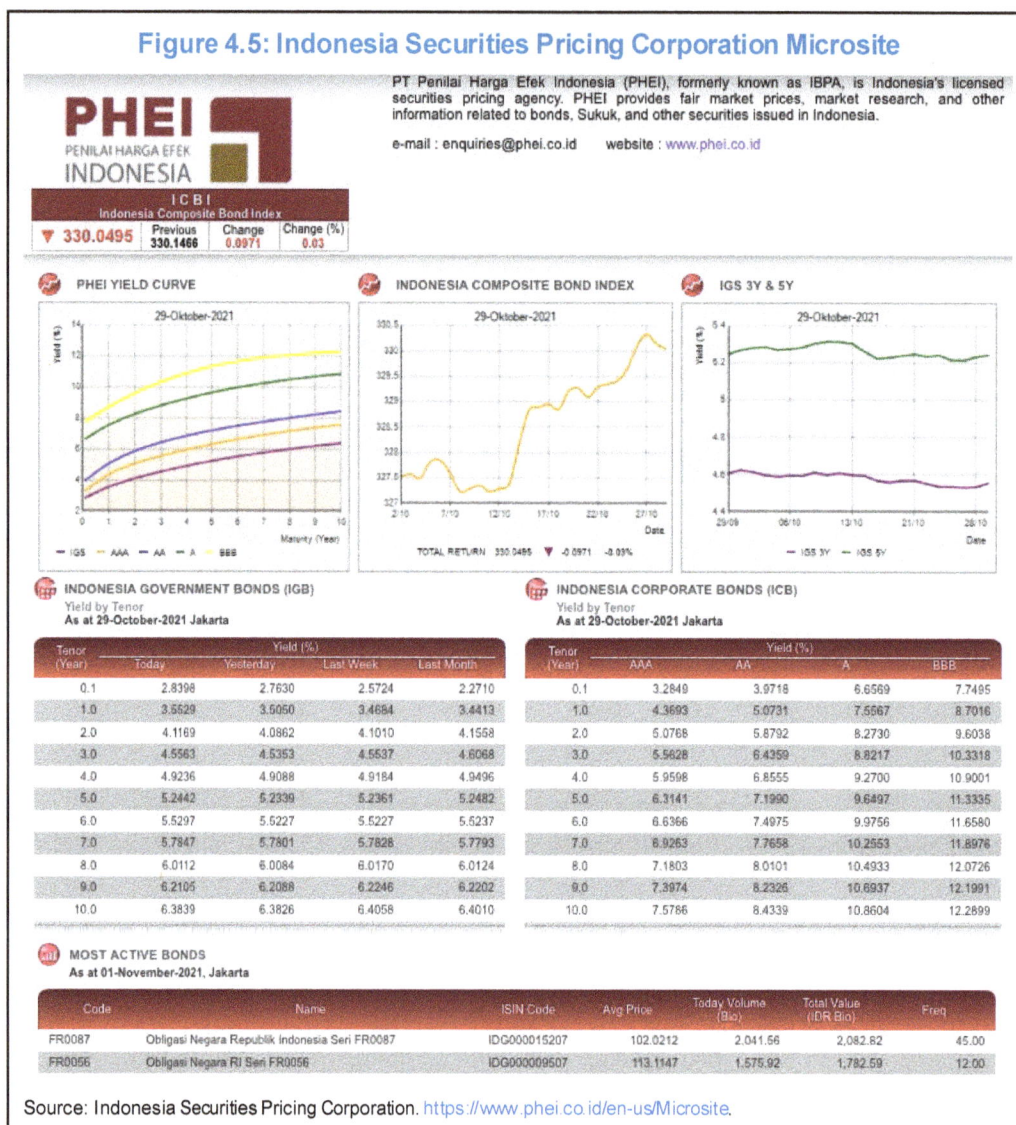

PT Penilai Harga Efek Indonesia (PHEI), formerly known as IBPA, is Indonesia's licensed securities pricing agency. PHEI provides fair market prices, market research, and other information related to bonds, Sukuk, and other securities issued in Indonesia.

e-mail : enquiries@phei.co.id   website : www.phei.co.id

**INDONESIA GOVERNMENT BONDS (IGB)**
Yield by Tenor
As at 29-October-2021 Jakarta

| Tenor (Year) | Yield (%) | | | |
|---|---|---|---|---|
| | Today | Yesterday | Last Week | Last Month |
| 0.1 | 2.8398 | 2.7630 | 2.5724 | 2.2710 |
| 1.0 | 3.5629 | 3.5050 | 3.4684 | 3.4413 |
| 2.0 | 4.1169 | 4.0862 | 4.1010 | 4.1558 |
| 3.0 | 4.5563 | 4.5353 | 4.5537 | 4.6068 |
| 4.0 | 4.9236 | 4.9088 | 4.9184 | 4.9496 |
| 5.0 | 5.2442 | 5.2339 | 5.2361 | 5.2482 |
| 6.0 | 5.5297 | 5.5227 | 5.5227 | 5.5237 |
| 7.0 | 5.7847 | 5.7801 | 5.7828 | 5.7793 |
| 8.0 | 6.0112 | 6.0084 | 6.0170 | 6.0124 |
| 9.0 | 6.2105 | 6.2088 | 6.2246 | 6.2202 |
| 10.0 | 6.3839 | 6.3826 | 6.4058 | 6.4010 |

**INDONESIA CORPORATE BONDS (ICB)**
Yield by Tenor
As at 29-October-2021 Jakarta

| Tenor (Year) | Yield (%) | | | |
|---|---|---|---|---|
| | AAA | AA | A | BBB |
| 0.1 | 3.2849 | 3.9718 | 6.6569 | 7.7495 |
| 1.0 | 4.3693 | 5.0731 | 7.5967 | 8.7016 |
| 2.0 | 5.0768 | 5.8792 | 8.2730 | 9.6038 |
| 3.0 | 5.5628 | 6.4359 | 8.8217 | 10.3318 |
| 4.0 | 5.9598 | 6.8555 | 9.2700 | 10.9001 |
| 5.0 | 6.3141 | 7.1990 | 9.6497 | 11.3335 |
| 6.0 | 6.6366 | 7.4975 | 9.9756 | 11.6580 |
| 7.0 | 6.9263 | 7.7658 | 10.2553 | 11.8976 |
| 8.0 | 7.1803 | 8.0101 | 10.4933 | 12.0726 |
| 9.0 | 7.3974 | 8.2326 | 10.6937 | 12.1991 |
| 10.0 | 7.5786 | 8.4339 | 10.8604 | 12.2899 |

**MOST ACTIVE BONDS**
As at 01-November-2021, Jakarta

| Code | Name | ISIN Code | Avg Price | Today Volume (Bio) | Total Value (IDR Bio) | Freq |
|---|---|---|---|---|---|---|
| FR0087 | Obligasi Negara Republik Indonesia Seri FR0087 | IDG000015207 | 102.0212 | 2.041.56 | 2,082.82 | 45.00 |
| FR0056 | Obligasi Negara RI Seri FR0056 | IDG000009507 | 113.1147 | 1.575.92 | 1,782.59 | 12.00 |

Source: Indonesia Securities Pricing Corporation. https://www.phei.co.id/en-us/Microsite.

## 2.  Bond Indexes in Indonesia

The Indonesia Bond Indexes were launched on 21 November 2014, following an initiative by OJK in conjunction with IDX and the then IBPA, to provide the Indonesian capital market with guidance on the performance of the bond market and its instruments. This was previously reported in the *ASEAN+3 Bond Market Guide for Indonesia* published in 2017.

Since then, these indexes have largely been referred to in PHEI publications, on the IDX website, and in other materials in the financial market media using the acronym INDOBeX.

## G.    Repo Market

### 4.    Triparty Repo Facility [NEW]

KPEI obtained OJK approval in July 2018 to act as third-party provider in triparty repo transactions. KPEI subsequently issued KPEI Regulation Number X-2 Regarding Triparty Repo Facility on 25 February 2019 to define its service provision and prescribe the rights and obligations of repo buyers and repo sellers.[34]

The KPEI regulation covers the procedures for the settlement on the purchase date and the repurchase date, and includes the substitution of securities. Both delivery-versus-payment and free-of-payment transactions are possible; for free-of-payment transactions, the transfer of funds occurs outside the triparty repo facility, but a confirmation of fund transfer is to be recorded in the triparty repo facility.

The repo business, the service provisions, and eligible participants follow the provisions in OJK Regulation No. 9/POJK.04/2015 Concerning Guidelines of Repurchase Agreement Transactions for Financial Services Institutions, as described in the *ASEAN+3 Bond Market Guide for Indonesia*.

While KPEI facilitates triparty repo transactions, it does not guarantee the repo transaction. KPEI provides maintenance and management of the margin, a mark-to-market service of the collateral, transaction settlement, and related activities. Margin is only available in the form of cash, as defined in the KPEI regulation. Eligible securities are securities as defined in the Capital Market Law.

As market standard, the Global Master Repurchase Agreement for Indonesia serves as the underlying agreement for repo transactions between counterparties; in addition, participants each need to execute a triparty repo facility agreement with KPEI.

## I.    Interest Rate and Fixed Income Futures

Just prior to the publication of the *ASEAN+3 Bond Market Guide for Indonesia*, IDX introduced the trading of bond futures contracts on the exchange market; this development was indicated in the bond market guide, but details could not be included in time. Hence, this section provides information on the two contracts directly relevant for the bond market.

The trading of futures contracts on IDX began in May 2017. Presently, four distinct contracts are being traded, two of which relate to the bond market. The legal and regulatory bases for futures and futures trading had been provisions in the Capital Market Law, which already recognized derivatives, and Bapepam Rule III.E.1 Concerning Futures Contract and Option on Securities or on Securities Index, dated 31 October 2003; OJK did not introduce new regulations at the time. IDX published its Rule Number II-M concerning Trading of Government Securities Futures Contracts on 25 April 2017 to facilitate the exchange-trading practices for the new instruments.

On 6 May 2020, OJK issued Regulation No. 32/POJK.04/2020 Concerning Securities Derivative Contracts, creating a single, comprehensive regulatory framework for securities derivatives. The regulation prescribes the need and process for OJK approval for each new derivatives product; the trading, clearing, and settlement of derivatives transactions; as well as participants and their obligations. The regulation covers trading of securities derivatives on both the exchange and alternative trading

---

[34] The text of the KPEI Regulation Number X-2 Triparty Repo Facility is available for download from the KPEI website at https://www.idclear.co.id/regulation/peraturan-triparty-repoen-US.

market (PPA), and the obligations of market trading and clearing institutions, including the need to publish derivatives-related information.

Subsequently, IDX published Rule Number II-E concerning Futures Contract Trading on 7 December 2020, which covered the trading hours of government bond futures contracts and transaction reporting times and practices, among other subjects. OJK Regulation No. 32/2020 also made necessary further adjustments to the trading provisions of futures contracts on exchange. The IDX rule was approved by OJK on 19 October 2020.

Trading hours for the bond futures contracts differ slightly from the normal exchange trading hours for debt securities (Table 4.2). Trading in session 1 starts and ends 30 minutes earlier, while session 2 is 45 minutes shorter. In contrast to normal exchange trading hours, there is no distinction between individual days of the week. In addition, the trading of futures contracts that are due ends at 3 p.m. on the last trading day for such contracts.

### Table 4.2: Indonesia Stock Exchange—Bond Futures Trading Hours

| Day | Session 1 | Session 2 |
|-----|-----------|-----------|
| Monday–Friday | 9 a.m. – 11.30 a.m. | 1:30 p.m. – 3.15 p.m. |

Note: Times given are for the Western Indonesian time zone in which Jakarta is located.
Source: Indonesia Stock Exchange. Products > Derivatives. https://www.idx.co.id/en-us/products/derivatives/.

Information on the bond futures contracts, including trading activity, market summary, and most active contracts are provided on the IDX website (Figure 4.7).

Like all exchange-traded instruments, transactions in bond futures on IDX are cleared by KPEI. KPEI issued Regulation Number III-3 on Clearing and Guarantee of Government Bond Futures Contracts on 26 April 2017 and updated its Regulation Number III-2 on Clearing and Guarantee of Settlement of Securities Futures Contract Transactions on 27 November 2020.[35] For the relevant regulations governing the obligations of clearing members on securities futures contract transactions, KPEI had previously issued Regulation Number III-1 on Clearing Members Obtaining Clearing and Guarantee Services of Futures Contract and Option Transaction Settlement on 23 November 2015. Please see the KPEI website for further details on these regulations.[36]

As the settlement of futures contracts occurs in cash, there is no involvement of KSEI in the settlement process.

---

[35] KPEI Regulation Number III-3 on Clearing and Guarantee of Government Bond Futures Contracts is available for download, presently only in Bahasa Indonesia, from the KPEI website at https://www.kpei.co.id/Media/Default/Regulations/Derivatif/PERATURAN%20KPEI%20NO%20III-3.PDF. KPEI Regulation Number III-2 on Clearing and Guarantee for Settlement of Securities Futures Contract Transactions is available, presently only in Bahasa Indonesia, from the KPEI website at https://www.idclear.co.id/Media/Default/Regulations/Derivatif/Peraturan%20KPEI%20No%20III-2_2020.PDF.
[36] KPEI Regulation Number III-1 on Clearing Members Obtaining Clearing and Guarantee Services of Futures Contract and Option Transaction Settlement is available, from the KPEI website, at https://www.idclear.co.id/Media/Default/Regulations/Derivatif/KPEI%20Rule%20No%20III-1.pdf.

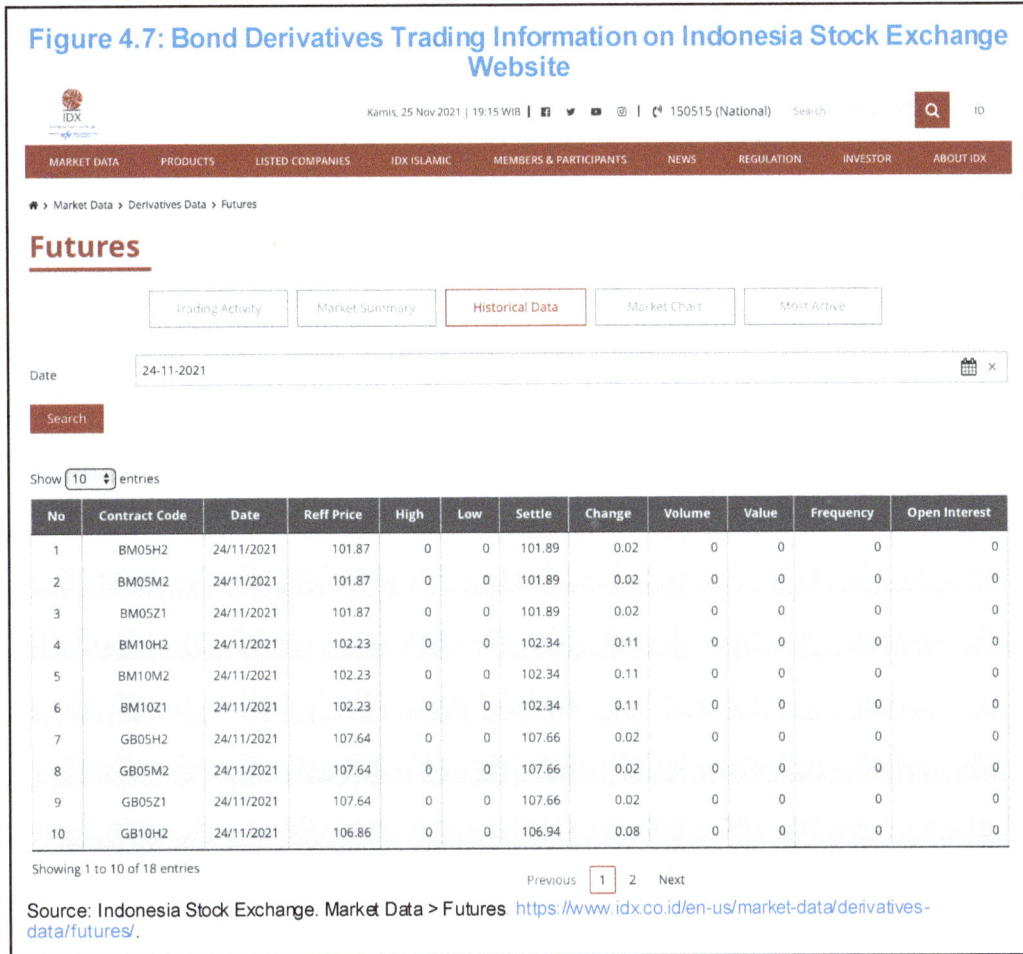

Figure 4.7: Bond Derivatives Trading Information on Indonesia Stock Exchange Website

Source: Indonesia Stock Exchange. Market Data > Futures. https://www.idx.co.id/en-us/market-data/derivatives-data/futures/.

### 1.    Indonesia Government Bond Futures [NEW]

IDX introduced Indonesia Government Bond Futures (IGBF) contracts to the exchange market on 8 May 2017 given the large amount of outstanding sovereign bonds. IGBF contracts are intended as a hedging instrument for primary dealers of government bonds.

IGBF contracts use benchmark government bonds with 5-year and 10-year tenors as the underlying instruments; hence, the contracts are designated as BM05 and BM10, respectively.

The contract has a value of IDR1 billion (or multiples thereof) and is quoted by price, with ticks at 1 basis point representing the actual price; rounding (e.g., to the nearest 5 basis points) is not practiced. Maturity dates for the IGBF contracts fall on the last trading day in March, June, September, and December. Cash settlement for IGBF contracts is on T+1.

More information on IGBF contracts can be found on the IDX website.[37]

### 2.    Basket Bond Futures [NEW]

Basket Bond Futures (BBF) contracts were introduced by IDX on 7 December 2020.

---

[37] See https://www.idx.co.id/en-us/products/derivatives/.

BBF represent a futures contract on the basis of a basket of government bonds with maturities between 4 years and less than 7 years for the 5-year contract (GB05MY), and maturities between 7 years and less than 11 years for the 10-year contract (GB10MY). Each basket contains three government bonds with the appropriate residual tenors that are selected by IDX on the basis of the largest amount outstanding and other considerations.

The contract value is IDR1 billion (or multiples thereof), with a tick size of 1 basis point (0.01%). BBF are settled in cash on T+1. The equivalent of 0.03 basis points of each transaction value in BBF are allocated to the Exchange Guarantee Fund.[38]

More information on BBF is available from the IDX webpage on derivatives.[39]

---

[38] The Exchange Guarantee Fund collects contributions from exchange member transactions to ensure fulfillment of obligations in the event of clearing member default.
[39] See https://www.idx.co.id/en-us/products/derivatives/.

# Bond Market Costs and Taxation

Changes related to bond market costs and taxation detailed in this update focus on the most recent changes to tax rates and taxation practices in the Indonesian bond market.

At the same time, the Government of Indonesia and market institutions have been known to introduce incentives, including fee reductions and waivers, to support market participants and business activities as part of their responses to the COVID-19 pandemic. Some of these incentives may be transitional or temporary. Interested parties are encouraged to confirm the applicability of market rates, fees, and charges detailed in the *ASEAN+3 Bond Market Guide for Indonesia*.

OJK, based on the Board of Commissioners Decree No. 24/KDK.01/2018 of 31 December 2018 Concerning Adjustment of the Registration Fee for Public Offering of Green Bonds, adjusted the registration fee to 25% of the rate specified in the Annex of the Government Regulation Number 11 of 2014, which stipulates the registration fee for the public offering of bonds in general. Hence, the registration fee for green bonds is 75% lower than the normal rate. This incentive applies from the time the decree is enacted until it is regulated differently at a later date.

In addition, in its Board of Directors Decree No. Kep-00038/BEI/05-2020 of 20 May 2020, IDX provided for a 50% reduction of the annual listing fee for green bonds. This incentive applies to the annual listing fee for a period of 5 years since the decree came into force.

## H.    Taxation Framework and Requirements

The Government of Indonesia promulgated the first Omnibus Law (formally Law No. 11 of 2020, also referred to as the Job Creation Law) on 2 November 2020, which contained measures affecting the taxation of bond interest for nonresident investors as well as taxation procedures for all investors. The corresponding implementing regulations were issued on 2 February 2021 (Government Regulation Number 9/2021) and on 18 February 2021 (MOF Regulation Number 18/PMK.03/2021). The relevant changes are detailed here in the context of the subjects included in the *ASEAN+3 Bond Market Guide for Indonesia*.

### 2.    Withholding Tax

Provisions in the Job Creation Law included a reduction of the standard withholding tax rate on interest, profit sharing, or similar income from bonds and *sukuk* for nonresidents from 20% to 10%, unless an applicable treaty rate is lower.

This revised standard rate is effective from 1 August 2021 and applies to interest from government, quasi-government, and corporate bonds and notes, including those issued via private placement, and is also applicable to profit sharing from Sharia-compliant instruments by these issuers or offerors.

Bond interest, a profit-sharing rate, or similar income for *sukuk* include the nominal interest or rate of the bond as well as differences between the sale price and acquisition price of the bond.

### 7.    Tax Concessions or Exemptions for Nonresident Investors

The reduction of the standard withholding tax rate from 20% to 10% (see section 2 of this chapter) represents a concession for nonresident investors and reflects the policy objective of the Government of Indonesia to further broaden its investor base, including through the active participation of nonresidents in the bond market.

### 8.    Changes in Tax Procedures [NEW]

While tax procedures in a given market, including the actual withholding process and underlying prescriptions, are typically not reviewed in detail in an *ASEAN+3 Bond Market Guide*, the tax procedures in Indonesia have typically required significant attention from nonresident investors and interested parties. As such, this update note provides information on notable changes with regard to the provision of tax information by investors into the Indonesian bond market.

The most recent notable changes in prescriptions or procedures for tax processing since 2018 include the following:

- Regulation of the Director General of Taxes Number PER-25/PJ/2018 Regarding the Procedure for the Application of Approval on the Avoidance of Double Taxation (often referred to as PER-25/PJ/2018), dated 21 November 2018 and effective 1 January 2019; and

- KSEI Circular Letter No. SE-0002/DIR-EKS/KSEI/0419 Regarding the Procedure for the Application of Approval on the Avoidance of Double Taxation and the Implementation of Corporate Action in KSEI, issued on 23 April 2019 and effective 13 May 2019. This circular letter replaced the earlier Circular Letter Regarding the Procedure for the Delivery of Domicile Letter for Foreign Taxpayer at KSEI issued in March 2015.

The DGT regulation was issued following market lobbying efforts, particularly to simplify the applicable forms and allow the submission of evidence in electronic form. In turn, KSEI, as a typical withholding agent for debt securities, simplified its procedure for account holders with the help of the streamlined DGT forms and process.

DGT now only requires a single form for all entities, with investors able to submit one form for up to 12 months, regardless of calendar year; the form no longer requires the details of specific income events or the withholding agent details; in addition, a certificate of residence instead of an authorization from the nonresident's domicile's tax authority is acceptable as proof of tax status.

DGT and, consequently, KSEI now accept evidence of an investor's tax status in electronic form, and investors can email KSEI with a cover letter and the softcopy of the documentary evidence; specific cut-off times for the submission have to be observed. DGT permitted documentary evidence in English through a regulation change in 2017.

In relation to the DGT form submitted, KSEI will not carry out any verification of the conformity or correctness of the form itself; the account holder remains responsible for any consequences arising from noncompliance or mistakes. However, similar to an instance where a submission deadline for the DGT form was missed, the investor has the opportunity to pursue any difference in applicable taxes through the tax reclaim process.

# Market Size and Statistics

The original *ASEAN+3 Bond Market Guide* was published in January 2012 and included several pages of Indonesian bond market statistics, including historical data such as bond holdings, bondholder distribution, outstanding amounts, and trading volumes. Not surprisingly, these data became stale soon after publication.

Hence, a chapter comprising bond market statistics has been discontinued. In the *ASEAN+3 Bond Market Guide for Indonesia* published in 2017, this chapter was replaced with a list of recommended sources for detailed, accurate, and current information sources on the Indonesian bond market. These sources have been updated below in alphabetical order.

- *AsianBondsOnline* (an ASEAN+3 initiative led by the Asian Development Bank)
  https://asianbondsonline.adb.org/economy/?economy=ID.
  - Market-at-a-Glance
  - Data (market size, yields, indicators, ratings, including historical data)
  - Market structure
  - Market summary
  - News (latest statistics)

- Bank Indonesia
  http://www.bi.go.id/en/moneter/Contents/Default.aspx.
  - Government bonds
  - Auction of Sertifikat Bank Indonesia
  - Auction of Bank Indonesia foreign exchange bills
  - Repo rates

- Indonesian Securities Pricing Corporation
  https://www.phei.co.id/en-us/.
  - Bond prices
  - Yield curves
  - Government and corporate bonds
  - Publications

- Indonesia Stock Exchange
  http://www.idx.co.id/en-us/home/marketinformation/bondsukuk/otctradereport.aspx.
  - Latest OTC trade report
  - Trade report summary
  - Most active securities
  - Government and corporate bonds

# VIII

# The Indonesian
# Islamic Bond Market

This chapter only contains relevant updates to instrument and issuance types in the Indonesian Islamic bond market; as such, not all sections included in the *ASEAN+3 Bond Market Guide for Indonesia* are reproduced in this update note.

## C.    Instruments in the Sharia Capital and Bond Markets

### 2.    Types of Sukuk

*Sukuk* may come in a number of different types, each representing a different underlying Islamic principle or a combination of these principles. Before a *sukuk* may be issued, it should get an opinion of Sharia compliance from a Sharia Capital Market Expert. Principally, the types of *sukuk* in existence are based on the Sharia Standard (No. 17) on Investment Sukuk issued by the Accounting and Auditing Organization for Islamic Financial Institutions, which is widely regarded as authoritative, and can be categorized as follows:[40]

(i)    Ownership Certificate on leased asset;
(II)   Ownership Certificate on benefit, which consist of Ownership Certificate on existing asset, Ownership Certificate on future asset, Ownership Certificate on party of services, Ownership Certificate on future services;
(iii)  Salam Certificate;
(iv)   Istishna Certificate;
(v)    Murabahah Certificate;
(vi)   Musyarakah Certificate;
(vii)  Muzara'a Certificate;
(viii) Musaqa Certificate; and
(ix)   Mugharasa Certificate.

*Sukuk ijarah* is the predominant type of *sukuk* being issued in the Indonesian market. Of the 53 corporate *sukuk* outstanding at the time of the compilation of the *ASEAN+3 Bond Market Guide for Indonesia*, 35 (68%) used an *Ijarah aqd* (Islamic contract).

### 3.    Green Sukuk [NEW]

The Government of Indonesia issues green *sukuk* as part of its *sukuk* issuance strategy under its global issuance program to finance the annual budget deficit. The amounts issued annually depend on budget financing needs, the issuance allocation to *sukuk*, as well as eligible green projects. The government also announced the issuance of green savings *sukuk* in 2021 under its *sukuk* issuance program. Similar to sovereign savings bonds, green savings *sukuk* are not tradeable and come with a floating interest rate (see also Chapter III.B for more details on these *sukuk* types).

---

[40] For detailed information, please see http://aaoifi.com/standards-under-review-4/?lang=en.

The Government of Indonesia, through the MOF, issued its first green *sukuk* in February 2018. The issuance was widely regarded as the first sovereign green *sukuk* globally. The MOF has since issued other tranches, both aimed at retail and institutional investors.

The green *sukuk* are issued in the form of *wakalah* certificates, which represent the contract of the *sukuk* holders with an agent that manages the underlying assets on behalf of the *sukuk* holders. The government has established a dedicated legal entity to issue sovereign *sukuk*.[41]

The issuance of green *sukuk* does not require the creation of a dedicated green *sukuk* framework. In formally adopting the ICMA Green Bond Principles (see link in Appendix 2), the Government of Indonesia issued its *Green Bond and Green Sukuk Framework* in 2018, which covers the eligibility criteria for the financing or refinancing of green projects via either green bonds or green *sukuk*. In addition, green *sukuk* have to comply with the prescriptions for Islamic instruments (see section 2 of this chapter).

The *Green Bond and Green Sukuk Framework* is available for download in English from the MOF website.[42]

### 4.    Cash Waqf Sukuk [NEW]

CWLS are Islamic bonds or *sukuk* linked to endowments (*waqf*). CWLS allow investors to buy *sukuk* that deliver coupons (hence, the mention of cash), as a type of donation, to organizations that administer endowment funds (*nadzir*), e.g., for social and welfare projects such as healthcare, education, and poverty alleviation. Investors in CWLS receive back their principal investment upon maturity or have the option to assign the principal to endowment organizations.

Endowment-linked *sukuk*, which are also referred to in Bahasa Indonesia as *sukuk wakaf*, may be offered in variants for institutional investors and for retail investors (*sukuk wakaf ritel*). Issuance size may depend on the type and number of endowments that are linked.

The first CWLS was issued on 10 March 2020, and the Government of Indonesia has so far issued three series of CWLS via a variation of private placements and using online and offline book-building exercises. Some details are provided below for illustration.

SW001, the first CWLS of its kind, was issued on 10 March 2020, via a private placement aimed at institutional investors; the issuance volume reached IDR50.85 billion, and issuance occurred at a discount. The discount was used to develop a retina center at Ahmad Wardi Waqf Hospital in Serang, Banten Province, while coupons are used to provide free cataract surgery for poor people.

SWR001, the first retail CWLS, was issued on 26 November 2020 with a 2-year tenor and an issuance amount of IDR14.91 billion from 1,041 investors, both retail and corporate. SWR001 was issued at par, and coupons are distributed to several social projects managed by *nadzir*, including housing and medical aid for the poor.

---

[41] Adapted by the ASEAN+3 Bond Market Forum Sub-Forum 1 team, based on publicly available information.
[42] Government of Indonesia. 2018. *Green Bond and Green Sukuk Framework*. https://www.djppr.kemenkeu. go.id/uploads/files/dmodata/in/6Publikasi/Offering%20Circular/ROI%20Green%20Bond%20and%20Green% 20Sukuk%20Framework.pdf.

The second retail CWLS, SWR002, was issued on 9 June 2021 with a 4-year tenor and in the amount of IDR24.14 billion to 591 investors. The underlying projects include mobile clinics and screening, medical services, and scholarships for the poor.

Please see also Chapter III.B in this update note for more information on the nature of CWLS as a debt instrument. Updated information in Bahasa Indonesia on the latest CWLS can be found on a dedicated webpage of the MOF.[43]

---

[43] See https://www.kemenkeu.go.id/single-page/sukuk-wakaf/.

# Recent Developments and Future Direction

## A.    Recent Major Developments

Recent major developments are considered those that occurred in the Indonesian bond market since the publication of the *ASEAN+3 Bond Market Guide for Indonesia* in August 2017. For easy reference, the developments are reflected in descending chronological order.

### 1.    Publication of Sustainable Development Goals Government Securities Framework and First Bond Issuance (2021) [NEW]

The Government of Indonesia has developed its *SDG Government Securities Framework*, a comprehensive framework that will cover the various aspects of sustainable financing, including green, social, and blue financing. The *SDG Government Securities Framework* will serve as guidance for sovereign issuances of green and blue social and sustainability bonds and *sukuk* that will fund eligible projects delivering environmental and social benefits in line with the Indonesian 2030 development agenda. The framework and its second-party opinion from CICERO and the International Institute for Sustainable Development were published in September 2021.[44]

The Government of Indonesia issued its first Republic of Indonesia SDG Bond on 23 September 2021. Representing another milestone for sovereign bonds, the bond was the first ever EUR-denominated SDG bond in the Securities and Exchange Commission-registered, shelf take-down format. The transaction was also one of the first conventional SDG bond issuances in Asia, reflecting Indonesia's leadership in sustainable financing and a significant step toward achieving the SDGs.[45]

### 2.    Reduction of Withholding Tax Rate for Debt Securities (2021) [NEW]

The Government of Indonesia promulgated the Job Creation Law (formally Law No. 11 of 2020) on 2 November 2020 and subsequently issued implementing regulations on 2 February 2021, which clarified aspects relevant for the bond market.

These aspects include a reduction of withholding tax on bond interest for nonresident bondholders from 20% to 10%, or an applicable tax treaty rate if lower. The bond interest rate reduction became effective on 2 August 2021, which was 6 months after the date of the regulation issuance.

Please also see Chapter VI.H for details on the new law and implementing regulations and the validity of the changes.

---

[44] The framework and its second-party opinion can be accessed via the MOF website at https://www.djppr.kemenkeu.go.id/page/load/3229.

[45] More information on the SGD bond may be found in the official press release, which is available at https://www.djppr.kemenkeu.go.id/page/load/3234.

### 3.    Launch of the Sustainable Finance Roadmap Phase II (2021–2025) [NEW]

OJK launched the *Sustainable Finance Roadmap Phase II (2021–2025)* on 15 January 2021 to build on the successful implementation of key milestones in Phase I, which ran from 2015 to 2019 and included the promulgation of green bond regulations in 2017, among many other subjects.

The updated *Sustainable Finance Roadmap Phase II (2021–2025)* includes plans for the development of a complete market ecosystem for sustainable finance and the definition of an appropriate taxonomy in conjunction with other institutions. It also hopes to address the limited research into sustainable finance and the lack of human resources dedicated to assessing and verifying green and other sustainable finance projects.

The text of the *Sustainable Finance Roadmap Phase II (2021–2025)* is available in English and can be downloaded from the OJK website.[46]

In 2020, OJK also became a member of the Network for Greening the Financial System.[47]

### 4.    Debt Securities or Sukuk Offering through Crowdfunding Services Based on Information Technology (2020) [NEW]

On 13 December 2020, OJK promulgated Regulation No. 57/POJK.04/2020 Offering of Securities through Crowdfunding Services Based on Information Technology; the regulation was subsequently further updated through OJK Regulation No. 16/POJK.04/2021 promulgated in August 2021. While the regulation of crowdfunding for securities offerings was not new—the original regulation was issued in December 2018 and focused on share offerings—the updated regulations expanded the scope of securities offerings via crowdfunding to include offerings of debt securities or *sukuk*. At the time of the initial introduction, crowdfunding had already been recognized for providing a fast, easy, and affordable alternative source of funding for start-ups and small and medium-sized enterprises that are not yet bankable to develop their business.[48]

The purpose of OJK introducing and expanding these crowdfunding regulations was to establish legal certainty and protection for platform organizers, offerors, and investors, and to ensure the use of reliable technology as well as appropriate information transparency of these activities in the capital market.

The regulation prescribes the licensing requirements for crowdfunding organizers, carries eligibility criteria for platforms and offerors, and sets the obligations of investors. Debt securities or *sukuk* issued via crowdfunding have to adhere to a number of specific requirements. The maximum amount to be raised is limited to IDR10 billion within 12 months, and the offering would need to be completed within that period; the maximum tenor is 2 years.

---

[46] OJK. 2021. *Sustainable Finance Roadmap Phase II (2021–2025)*. https://www.ojk.go.id/id/berita-dan-kegiatan/publikasi/Documents/Pages/Roadmap-Keuangan-Berkelanjutan-Tahap-II-%282021-2025%29/Roadmap%20Keuangan%20Berkelanjutan%20Tahap%20II%20%282021-2025%29.pdf.

[47] The Network for Greening the Financial System's purpose is to help strengthen the global response required to meet the goals of the Paris Agreement and to enhance the role of the financial system to manage risks and mobilize capital for green and low-carbon investments in the broader context of environmentally sustainable development. To this end, the network defines and promotes best practices to be implemented within and outside of the membership of the network, and it conducts or commissions analytical work on green finance. For further information, please see https://www.ngfs.net/en.

[48] Information provided by KSEI and adapted from reports in the public domain.

KSEI has been working with crowdfunding organizers to establish connectivity and procedures for the registration of the issued debt securities or *sukuk* and their ownership once the issuance is complete.

Please see Chapter III.E for a detailed description of debt securities issuance via crowdfunding platforms.

### 5.    Indonesia Stock Exchange Launched Alternative Trading Platform (2020) [NEW]

On 7 November 2020, IDX launched SPPA as an OTC trading platform for bonds and *sukuk* in the secondary market. SPPA was the result of further developing ETP (see Chapter IV.B.5 in the *ASEAN+3 Bond Market Guide for Indonesia*), but it represents an entirely new system.

OJK had issued the underlying OJK Regulation No. 8/POJK.04/2019 Concerning Alternative Market Organizers (which are referred to as PPA) in 2019 and had previously licensed IDX as an entity qualified to operate a PPA. IDX operates SPPA as a platform distinct from its exchange market. Details on SPPA can be found in Chapter IV.B.6 in this update note.

### 6.    Launch and Expansion of eASY.KSEI Application (2020) [NEW]

On 20 April 2020, KSEI launched its facility to support general meetings of shareholders of public limited liability companies with shares deposited at KSEI. The application, referred to as eASY.KSEI, will be implemented in two phases: (i) the e-proxy module, which will electronically facilitate and integrate the granting of authority by shareholders to an authorized representative, and (ii) the e-voting module to electronically facilitate the attendance and voting process during a general meeting so shareholders can participate in the meeting without the need for physical attendance.

The launch had been under preparation for some time and was eventually brought forward to support the Government of Indonesia's response to the COVID-19 pandemic.

KSEI's annual general meeting of shareholders on 28 June 2021 was the first general meeting to utilize both the e-proxy and e-voting modules in the eASY.KSEI application. The application is also complimented with a general meeting broadcast module that provides viewing through a Zoom webinar format via the AKSes facility on the KSEI website.[49]

The development is mentioned here because the platform is intended to also be used for bondholder meetings in the future. Please see section B for information on the future expansion of the eASY.KSEI application.

### 7.    Introduction of Sustainability Bonds (2019) [NEW]

BRI issued the first sustainability bond by a financial services institution in Indonesia (and in Southeast Asia) in March 2019. Proceeds from the 5-year bond were allocated toward a combination of green and social projects including housing subsidies; micro-, small-, and medium-sized enterprise empowerment; green buildings; and low-carbon transportation in Indonesia.

Please see Chapter III.B.4 for details on BRI's sustainability bond and similar instrument types in the Indonesian market and their underlying frameworks.

---

[49] The KSEI announcement in relation to its 2021 general meeting of shareholders is available for download at https://www.ksei.co.id/Announcement/Files/128657_ksei_4012_dir_0521_202106032030.pdf.

### 8. Introduction of Private Placement Regulation (2019) [NEW]

OJK issued OJK Regulation No. 30/POJK.04/2019 Concerning Issuance of Debt Securities and/or Sukuk Not Through a Public Offering (private placement regulation) on 29 November 2019. The regulation brought the issuance of debt securities or *sukuk* via private placement under the purview of OJK. It contains eligibility criteria for entities wishing to issue a private placement as well as other prescriptions for the debt securities or *sukuk* and the issuance process. The regulation came into effect on 1 June 2020.

In contrast to public offerings of debt securities or *sukuk*, private placements do not require registration with and approval of OJK. The regulation was not intended to change existing market practices but to bring the existing private placement market segment under the regulatory coverage of OJK, provide issuing entities and investors with legal certainty, and tighten eligibility and investor protection practices.

Private placement as a method of issuance in the Indonesian bond market is described in Chapter III.E. For detailed information on the issuance process of private placements under the new regulation, please see Chapter II.F.5.

### 9. Use of Central Bank Money for Settlement of Securities Transactions (2019) [NEW]

Since 22 July 2019, cash settlement of securities transactions to be settled at KSEI has been carried out using central bank money. This achievement is generally referred to in the Indonesian market as "Full CeBM."

Before Full CeBM was implemented, KSEI account holders—custodian banks and securities companies—had to conduct cash settlement for securities transactions through commercial banks appointed by KSEI as payment banks.

The implementation of Full CeBM is in accordance with the Principles of Financial Market Infrastructures issued by the Committee on Payment and Market Infrastructures and the International Organization of Securities Commissions.[50]

### 10. Introduction of the Professional Investors Concept (2018) [NEW]

With the promulgation of the Public Offering to Professional Investors Regulation (OJK Regulation No. 11/POJK.04/2018) on 1 August 2018, with effect that same day, OJK introduced to the Indonesian capital market a formal definition for professional investors.

Kindly refer to Chapter III.N in this update note for a complete description of the professional investors concept, eligibility criteria, and setting of selling and transfer restrictions.

### 11. Introduction of T+2 Settlement for Exchange Transactions (2018) [NEW]

The Indonesian capital market successfully implemented T+2 settlement for transactions executed on IDX with effect from 23 November 2018. This includes fixed-income transactions executed on IDX.

From 2016 to 2018, IDX conducted studies, distributed questionnaires, conducted focus group discussions, organized self-assessments, and held meetings with IDX members, custodian banks, payment banks, and system application providers—as

---

[50] Adapted from KSEI. 2019. *Annual Report 2019*. https://www.ksei.co.id/annual-reports.

well as local, foreign, retail, and institutional customers—in preparation for the shortening from the original T+3 settlement cycle.

In addition to benefiting the Indonesian capital market in terms of competitiveness and credibility, the change was aimed at harmonizing settlement cycles among exchanges globally. The change itself was made possible by the increasing integration of information technology systems, including the use of a SID and a customer funds account, which allows for a faster allocation and settlement process.

### 12.    Issuance of First-Ever Sovereign Green Sukuk (2018) [NEW]

The Government of Indonesia issued its first green *sukuk* in February 2018, following the adoption of the ICMA Green Bond Principles and the publication of its *Green Bond and Green Sukuk Framework*. The green *sukuk* was widely recognized as the first sovereign green *sukuk* globally.

The inclusion of green *sukuk* in the mix of sovereign debt instruments, and the recognition of eligible underlying green projects, is aimed at supporting the Government of Indonesia's greenhouse gas emissions reduction goal.[51]

Please see Chapter III.B and Chapter VIII of this update note for details on green bond and green *sukuk* types, respectively, as well as their characteristics. More information on the ICMA Green Bond Principles are available from the ICMA website.[52]

### 13.    Indonesia Stock Exchange Joined Climate Bonds Initiative Partner Program (2018) [NEW]

In February 2018, IDX became the first exchange in Southeast Asia to join the Climate Bonds Initiative Partner Program.

IDX was the sixth exchange to partner with the Climate Bonds Initiative in a diverse grouping that includes the London Stock Exchange, the Luxembourg Green Exchange, Deutsche Börse, Bolsa Mexicana, and Nasdaq Nordics. Participating exchanges are committed to playing a greater role in the development of global and national green finance, with a particular focus on green bonds.[53]

In July, IDX listed the first corporate green bond (see Chapter III.B for details).

## B.    Future Direction

### 1.    Future Development of SPRINT Platform [NEW]

SPRINT is envisaged to enter the next stage of development to enable the electronic submission of issuance documents for public offerings of bonds and *sukuk* through shelf registration (from the second tranche onward), issuance documents for public offerings of bonds and *sukuk* to professional investors, and issuance documents for private placements of bonds and *sukuk* (including medium-term notes).

---

[51] Statement adapted from *Indonesia's Green Bond and Green Sukuk Initiative* and prepared by the United Nations Development Programme Indonesia.
https://www.undp.org/content/dam/LECB/docs/pubs-reports/undp-ndcsp-green-sukuk-share.pdf.
[52] International Capital Market Association. 2018. *The Green Bond Principles*.
https://www.icmagroup.org/green-social-and-sustainability-bonds/green-bond-principles-gbp/.
[53] Information adapted from Climate Bonds Initiative press release available at https://www.climatebonds.net /2018/02/indonesia-idx-new-partnership-cbi-meanwhile-eba-pina-sign-new-mou-cbi-join-forces-green.

### 2.    Expansion of e-IPO Service [NEW]

Following the launch of Electronic Indonesia Public Offering for equity securities, known as e-IPO, OJK and the market institutions IDX, IDClear, and KSEI are planning to expand e-IPO to public offerings of bonds and *sukuk*. An in-depth study will be carried out as a first step toward realizing this objective.

### 3.    Expansion of eASY.KSEI Platform to Include Bondholder Meetings [NEW]

Following the implementation of e-voting and live streaming of shareholder meetings in 2021, KSEI is hoping to expand its eASY.KSEI platform further by including functionality for bondholder meetings. Discussions with regulatory authorities and market stakeholders are ongoing.

# Appendix 2
# Resource Information

For easy reference and access to further information about the topics discussed in this update note, interested parties are encouraged to utilize the following links (all websites are available in English); items marked "[NEW]" were not included in the *ASEAN+3 Bond Market Guide for Indonesia* or have since changed.

ASEAN Capital Markets Forum—ASEAN Green Bond Standards [NEW]
https://www.theacmf.org/initiatives/sustainable-finance/asean-green-bond-standards.

ASEAN+3 Bond Market Guide—Indonesia (2017)
https://asianbondsonline.adb.org/abmg.php#ino-2017.

*AsianBondsOnline* (Asian Development Bank) [NEW]
https://asianbondsonline.adb.org/economy/?economy=ID.

*AsianBondsOnline* (Asian Development Bank)—Green Bonds [NEW]
https://asianbondsonline.adb.org/green-bonds/index.html.

Bank Indonesia
http://www.bi.go.id/en/Default.aspx.

Climate Bonds Initiative [NEW]
https://www.climatebonds.net.

Green Bond Principles (International Capital Market Association) [NEW]
https://www.icmagroup.org/green-social-and-sustainability-bonds/green-bond-principles-gbp/.

Financial Services Authority (Otoritas Jasa Keuangan)
http://www.ojk.go.id/en/Default.aspx.

Indonesia Central Securities Depository (Kustodian Sentral Efek Indonesia)
http://www.ksei.co.id/?setLocale=en-US.

Indonesia Clearing and Guarantee Corporation (Kliring Penjaminan Efek Indonesia)
https://www.idclear.co.id. [NEW]

Indonesia Securities Pricing Corporation (Penilai Harga Efek Indonesia)
https://www.phei.co.id/en-us/.

Indonesia Stock Exchange (Bursa Efek Indonesia)
http://www.idx.co.id/index-En.html.

Ministry of Finance—Green Bond and Green Sukuk Framework [NEW]
https://www.djppr.kemenkeu.go.id/uploads/files/dmodata/in/6Publikasi/Offering%20Circular/ROI%20Green%20Bond%20and%20Green%20Sukuk%20Framework.pdf.

# Appendix 3
# Glossary of Technical Terms

This glossary focuses on terms that appear in this update note. The ASEAN+3 Bond Market Forum supports the efforts by OJK to maintain specific terminology for roles and functions expressed in the Capital Market Law and subsidiary regulations. Hence, this glossary needs to include, in addition to their English translations, a number of terms in Bahasa Indonesia to illustrate the distinctions intended in the original versions of law and regulations, even though they may not always match terms applied in international market practice.

| | |
|---|---|
| *agen permantau* | Bahasa Indonesia for monitoring agent [NEW] |
| Alternative Trading Platform | Alternative trading venue developed and operated by IDX [NEW] |
| Alternative Market Organizer | Licensed operator of an alternative trading venue [NEW] |
| Bahasa | Typical shortening of Bahasa Indonesia, the national language |
| Bahasa Indonesia | The national language of Indonesia |
| Bapepam | Badan Pengawas Pasar Modal (Capital Market Supervisory Agency) (original name until 2005) |
| Bapepam-LK | Badan Pengawas Pasar Modal dan Lembaga Keuangan (Capital Market Supervisory Agency) (predecessor agency of OJK from 2005 until 2012) |
| bond futures | Financial derivatives requiring the purchase or sale of underlying debt securities or *sukuk* at a predetermined date for a predetermined price |
| crowdfunding | Funding of projects aimed at collecting small amounts from a large number of contributors—here through the issuance of securities—typically through electronic or Internet-based platforms [NEW] |
| crowdfunding organizer | Party licensed to and responsible for operating a crowdfunding platform [NEW] |
| Diaspora bond | Preliminary name of a planned sovereign bond type aimed at Indonesian citizens living abroad [NEW] |
| *emiten* | Specific term in Bahasa Indonesia for the issuer of a public offering of debt securities (see also English equivalent: Issuer) |
| endowment *sukuk* | Sharia-compliant instrument with returns aimed at supporting charitable causes [NEW] |
| filing | Action of submitting documentation for a private placement to OJK |
| financial institution | Institution in the financial market in Indonesia not supervised by OJK such as Bank Indonesia and the Indonesia Deposit Insurance Corporation |

| financial services institution | Institution carrying out activities in the banking sector, the capital market, insurance sector, or as a pension fund or financing institution, and supervised by OJK |
|---|---|
| Full CeBM | Describes the exclusive use of central bank money in the cash leg of securities transaction settlement at KSEI [NEW] |
| green bond | Bond that raises proceeds for environmental (green) projects or those aimed at combating climate change [NEW] |
| Green Bond Principles | A set of rules and criteria designating a green bond; developed and maintained by the International Capital Market Association [NEW] |
| green *sukuk* | Sharia instrument that raises proceeds for environmental (green) projects or those aimed at combating climate change [NEW] |
| IDClear | New branding and website name of KPEI (launched 8 April 2021) |
| IDXNet | Platform operated by IDX to receive and store disclosure information from public companies and issuers of listed debt securities; integrated with SPE to form SPE-IDXNet |
| INDOBeX | Acronym for Indonesia Bond Indexes |
| information memorandum | Key disclosure document for private placements |
| issuer | Specific term used in English translations of OJK regulations for a (corporate) entity issuing or having issued a public offering (of debt securities) that is still outstanding (see also Bahasa equivalent: *emiten*); in this update note, may also be used as a summary term for issuing entities if not relating to law and regulations |
| monitoring agent | A party who shall be a trust agent or bond trustee licensed by OJK and, in the context of a private placement, has a specific function to monitor the fulfillment of an offeror's obligation until maturity of the debt securities or *sukuk* issued via private placement [NEW] |
| *nadzir* | Islamic institution(s) or organization(s) responsible for endowment management |
| offeror | Any entity wishing to offer a private placement to professional investors (see also Bahasa equivalent: *penerbit*) [NEW] |
| Omnibus bill | Proposed legislation [NEW] |
| Omnibus law | Legislation to address overlapping regulations and create a conducive business and investment climate [NEW] |
| *penerbit* | Specific term in Bahasa Indonesia for an entity issuing a private placement; term is also used in the context of the issuance of sovereign retail *sukuk* (see also English equivalent: offeror) [NEW] |
| primary dealer | Commercial bank or securities company appointed by the MOF to purchase and onward sell debt securities or *sukuk* issued by the Government of Indonesia and its agencies |
| private placement | Method of issuance not through a public offering, with specific eligibility for issuing entities and limitation of investor types |
| professional investors | Term used in OJK regulations for the professional investor type in the Indonesian bond market [NEW] |
| prospectus | Key disclosure document for public offerings of debt securities, including for offerings of debt securities to professional investors |

| | |
|---|---|
| public offering | An offering of securities made by an issuer (domestic or foreign) within a certain time and specified amounts, either within the territory of Indonesia or to Indonesian citizens abroad, offered either through mass media or otherwise to more than 100 persons or resulting in sales to more than 50 persons |
| public offering to professional investors | Issuance of securities to professional investors only, with selected concessions for the issuer |
| registration | Refers to the registration of securities with KSEI to be eligible for settlement and safekeeping in the Indonesian market |
| selling restrictions | Provisions limiting the issuance or sale of debt securities or *sukuk* aimed only at professional investors to general investors |
| Sharia bond | Term for *sukuk* in the Indonesian market |
| SPE | Electronic reporting system for obligations under OJK capital market regulations; integrated with IDXNet for disclosure obligations under IDX listing rules to form SPE-IDXNet |
| SPRINT | Electronic system used by OJK to receive Registration Statements and supporting documents; integrated with IDX registration system for listing applications [NEW] |
| Securities Transaction Reporting Platform | Despite the name, electronic platform for the capture of OTC bond market transactions post-trade |
| *sukuk* | Debt instrument under Islamic principles; also Sharia bond |
| *sukuk ritel* | Bahasa Indonesia term for *sukuk* distributed to retail investors |
| *sukuk tabungan* | Bahasa Indonesia term for *sukuk* aimed at the improvement of the savings rate of individual Indonesian citizens |
| *sukuk wakaf* | Endowment-linked *sukuk* (transliterated from *waqf*) [NEW] |
| supplementary information memorandum | Key disclosure document for subsequent issuances in a continuous private placement |
| sustainability bond | Bond that raises proceeds for environmental (green) or social projects |
| transfer restrictions | Provisions limiting the transfer of debt securities or *sukuk* aimed only at professional investors to general investors |
| triparty repo facility | Service provided by KPEI to eligible financial services institutions |
| triparty repo facility agreement | Agreement to be signed with KPEI by eligible participants of the triparty repo service |
| *wakalah* | Islamic principle for the contract between an agent and *sukuk* holders where the agent administers the *sukuk*-underlying assets on behalf of the *sukuk* holders |
| *wali amanat* | Bahasa Indonesia term for a trust agent or bond trustee which, in the context of a private placement, has a specific function as a monitoring agent |
| *waqf* | Islamic endowment(s) [NEW] |
| *zakat* | Form of Islamic obligatory charity |

Source: ASEAN+3 Bond Market Forum Sub-Forum 1 team.

www.ingramcontent.com/pod-product-compliance
Lightning Source LLC
Chambersburg PA
CBHW050050220326
41599CB00045B/7355